THE FOX HERITAGE

PICTORIAL RESEARCH BY CAROLYN KELLOGG
"PARTNERS IN PROGRESS" BY TOM RICHARDS

SPONSORED BY FOX CITIES CHAMBER OF COMMERCE AND INDUSTRY

WINDSOR PUBLICATIONS, INC.
WOODLAND HILLS, CALIFORNIA

THE
FOX
HERITAGE

A HISTORY OF WISCONSIN'S FOX CITIES
BY ELLEN KORT

THIS BOOK IS DEDICATED TO MY PARENTS, TO MY CHILDREN AND MY CHILDREN'S CHILDREN. MAY THEY LEARN TO LOVE THE MAGIC AND LEGENDS OF THEIR OWN HISTORY.

All photos appear courtesy of the
Outagamie County Historical Society, Inc.,
unless otherwise indicated.

Publisher: John M. Phillips
Editorial Director: Corporate Biographies: Karen Story
Senior Picture Editor: Teri Davis Greenberg
Design Director: Alexander D'Anca
Marketing Director: Ellen Kettenbeil
Sales Coordinator: Joan Baker

Staff for *An Illustrated History of the Fox Cities*
Senior Editor: Jim Mather, F. Jill Charbonneau
Editor: Leslie King
Picture Editors: Laurel Paley, Michelle Hudun
Assistant Director Corporate Biographies: Phyllis Gray
Corporate Biographies Editor: Judith Hunter
Editorial Assistants: Kathy Brown, Patricia Buzard, Gail Koffman, Lonnie Pham, Pat Pittman
Sales Manager: Bob Moffitt
Sales Representative: Pat DeGroot

Designer: Ellen Ifrah

Library of Congress Cataloging in Publication Data

Kort, Ellen, 1936-
    An illustrated history of the Fox cities.

    Includes index.
    1. Fox River Valley (Wis.)—History. 2. Fox River Valley (Wis.)—Description and travel. 3. Fox River Valley (Wis.)—Industries. I. Title.
F587.F72K67   1984   977.5'39   84-21933
ISBN 0-89781-083-X

Contents

Acknowledgements

History, someone once said, is falling in love over and over again. May they learn to love the magic and legends of their own history. It is falling in love with a place, its people, the voices that call from the other side of centuries. The Fox River Valley has been my home for almost half of my life. I have walked some of its history, felt its heart beat, heard the song of its river. This book became for me, a work that was both exciting and consuming, fascinating and frustrating. Researching the hundreds of years of history that shaped seven communities was like running in tall grass. It demanded hard work, patience and concentration. Perhaps the most difficult task in preparing a book such as this, with its limitations of time and space, is choosing what to omit as well as what to include. It is my hope that it will whet your appetite to search for more, that it will cause you, too, to listen for the voices of the past, that it will inspire you to fall in love with the place you call home.

The Fox Cities Chamber of Commerce and Industry and Windsor Publications have made this book a reality and to them go my indebted thanks. Although it is impossible to name each person who made a contribution to this book, "The Fox Heritage" would not have been possible without the vision of Don Stone and the encouragement and sensitive editing provided by Jill Charboneau and Jim Mather. I'd also like to thank the resource libraries and the Outagamie County Historical Society for their personalized assistance and for allowing me to "camp out" in their local history departments. Bill Weiner became my research assistant when I needed him most and provided, not only valuable help, but an enthusiasm that was contagious.

My family and friends have been an important support group in this project and their encouragement and understanding kept me sane and helped me along the way. I'd also like to thank Carolyn Kellogg and Tom Richards who added the beauty and backbone to this book, and the "Partners in Progress" whose belief made the project possible.

Finally, a special salute to all the historians who have known and loved this valley.

Neenah's Riverside Park was illustrated in the 1880 volume, History of Winnebago County. *Courtesy, State Historical Society of Wisconsin (SHSW)*

Prologue

Over a million years ago, a vast shallow sea covered the central part of Wisconsin, including the entire Fox River Valley. Through a process of erosion and a heaving and settling of the earth, the land eventually rose above the water.

Later, huge ice masses moved southward through Wisconsin over what is now Lake Michigan. The glaciers spread into the Green Bay region and gouged out channels of the Fox and Wolf rivers. The origin of the opposite stream flow of these two rivers is buried in this geologic past. Some geologists believe that the upper Fox River once drained into the Wisconsin River. They believe that the level of the land may slowly have changed, elevating one end of the valley and lowering the northeastern part. The melting glacier formed a large lake, overflowed, and found the course of the lower Fox River leaving only the low divide at Portage, Wisconsin to separate the valleys of these two opposite-flowing streams.

This natural water route connecting the Mississippi and the St. Lawrence River basins would carry Indians, trappers, missionaries, and settlers to a land rich with promise. To know the Fox River is to know the history of this valley, for the river is the thread that weaves one generation to another in the tapestry of our Fox Cities heritage.

The Charles A. Grignon "Mansion in the Woods," seen at right in this pastoral scene, was the only resting spot for travelers between Green Bay and Lake Winnebago in the early 1800s.

The Journey

As dawn broke on the Fox River, slivers of sunlight penetrated the mist that covered the water. The man and his birch bark canoe emerged from the mist—united in one dark shape—at home on the river. Moments before, he sprinkled tobacco on the water, to compensate for trespassing and to allow him safe passage over this watery pathway.

The year was 1634. The imaginary traveler—a Winnebago Indian who believed the Fox River had been given to him by a water spirit called "Wak'tcex-i". His Fox was a wilderness river with crashing

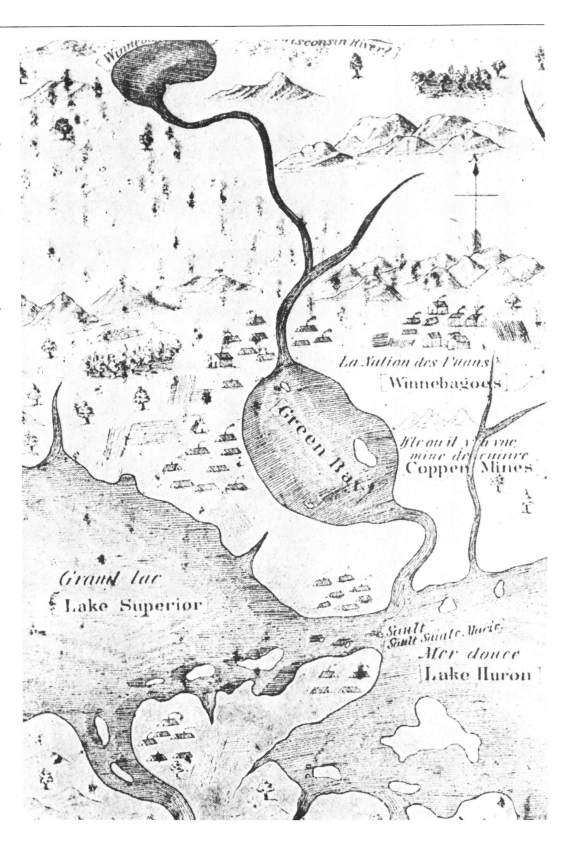

waterfalls and rapids, a current
swift and wild, and gorges of jagged rock.
Its waters were filled with leaping sturgeon
and trout. Its quiet, gentle inlets were safe
for ducks and geese, beavers and muskrat.

THE INDIANS

Because the Fox River Valley was a place
of natural beauty savored by the Indians, it
became a gathering place for many tribes.
Legends say that ducks and pigeons were
so plentiful that the Indians caught them
in nets as they landed for food, and
sturgeon were speared as they struggled up
river to spawn. Rich valley soil yielded
harvests of corn, pumpkin, mellons, squash,

and tobacco for these first farmers. Wild
grapes, plums, apples, and nuts were easy
to gather and the Indians were the early
masters of maple sugaring. Forest animals
furnished a seemingly limitless supply of
fresh meat and skins for clothing.

Three great Indian nations have figured
more than any others in the history of the
Fox River Valley: The Dakotah (a Sioux
tribe of the western plains), the
Algonquian (a tribe originating in the
Ottawa River valley in Canada), and the
Iroquois (confederacy of tribes from central
New York). The Sioux tribes seemed to
have lived in the Fox Valley long before
the coming of the first white man. Most of

Seth Eastman documented a Winnebago settlement for the book Information Respecting the History, Conditions, and Prospect of Indian Tribes of the United States, *published in the mid-1800s. SHSW*

An 1842 lithograph shows a Menominee village at present Green Bay, published in Paris in Vues et Souvenirs de l'Amerique du Nord *by Francis (Comte) de Castelnan. The Menominee are the oldest tribe of Great Lakes Indians in Wisconsin, believed to be descended from prehistoric Woodland Indians. SHSW*

the Algonquian tribes came to the valley later, in flight from the warring Iroquois. The Iroquois never actually called Wisconsin home, but their aggression had a powerful and tragic effect on Wisconsin history.

Because of the protection of Lake Michigan, only Wisconsin and the upper peninsula of Michigan were safe from Iroquois attack. Driven from their eastern lands by the Iroquois, the natural waterways of the Fox River and the lushness of its valley provided a haven for the Algonquians. In time, the Algonquian tribes of Sauk, Fox, Mascoutin, Kickapoo,

and Potawatomi came to live on the Fox.

The lower Fox River Valley was the home of the Winnebago tribe, part of the great Sioux nation who, according to Indian legend migrated from Mexico. Early Neenah-Menasha historian Publius Lawson made a study of the Winnebago people and traced their migration from the southern part of the Virginias and Carolinas and along the Ohio valley.

The Menominee Indians, part of the Algonquian tribe, are direct descendants of early Woodland Indians. They claim, in their sacred lore, to originate from a great bear which emerged at the mouth of the

Menominee River but early traders suggested that they had been driven from the east by the Iroquois. The only tribe to live in peace with the Winnebago, the French called the Menominee "folles avoines" or "wild oat eaters" because the tribe harvested the wild rice that grew in abundance in the shallow portions of small lakes and rivers. But the Algonquian name wild rice was "ma·no·min" and the tribe came to be called Menominee. The oldest

Outagami meant "dwellers on the other shore" to the native tribe. Labeled as cunning, clever, restless, and aggressive by historians, the Outagami carried the totem of the hawk from which they claimed descent. Known as a strongly independent renegade tribe, the Fox came to Wisconsin and the valley from lower Michigan.

One trader described the Outagami as "large, with disagreeable faces, brutish voices and evil aspects". Other early

Algonquian tribe in Wisconsin, the Menominee were considered to be loyal and dependable by the white man. Many an early French trader and white settler owed his life to the friendship of the Menominee. The Menominee are the oldest known continuous residents in Wisconsin. They remain exclusively a Wisconsin tribe and still occupy a small northern portion of their original homeland.

Most of the color in the early history of the Fox River Valley comes from the Fox or Outagami Indians, called "les renards" by the French and Fox by the English.

travelers spoke of them "as arrogant and quarrelsome". The Fox refused to be influenced by the French or submissive to the white man, and war stories and tales of their courage and defiance became legendary. So determined were they to hold on to their own way of life, they disrupted the French fur trade for two generations in an attempt to drive the foreigners from the valley.

Siouan people traveled in colonies, and like most Indian migrations made slow and difficult progress with no specific destination in mind. The migration was often interrupted when good hunting

The Mesquaki Indians, whose nicknames "Outagamie" and "Fox" would name a county and a river, came from lower Michigan about 1650, building a village on the west bank of the Wolf River, one mile west of present-day Leeman. This photo, taken by George R. Fox around 1915, shows outlined in white lime the archaeological ruins of the gardens of the Fox village, called Ouestatenong. Photo by George R. Fox. SHSW

James Lewis' The Aboriginal Portfolio *of 1835 included this portrait of Fox Chief Cut-taa-tas-tia. SHSW*

grounds were discovered, or when it became necessary to fight off another tribe. After crossing the Allegheny Mountains the Winnebago most likely followed the Ohio River, crossed the present state of Illinois to the mouth of the Missouri, and followed the Mississippi to the "Great Water" of Lake Michigan. They eventually drifted into Wisconsin and made their home near Lake Winnebago.

Samuel de Champlain's map of 1532 shows them as a nation of "Puans", living near a lake of "stinking fish". A Menominee Indian legend of the term "Puan" comes from the "pole cat" skins the Winnebago wore. But the tribe of many names may have finally become Winnebago by the French translation of their original Siouan name "Ovenibigontz" (People of the Original Speech).

Early writers tell of the savagery and cruelty of the Winnebagos, of their struggle for existence, their treachery and cannibalism. Lawson described them as "the most filthy, most obstinate and bravest people of any Indian tribe."

Although each of these Indian tribes was unique in customs and temperament, all shared a oneness with the natural world of the wilderness. Their sense of time came from the seasons and the land. They gave respect to Mother Earth for beauty and nourishment and to Father Sun for the wind, rain, thunder and lightning.

Outagamie...Kaukauna...Menasha...Winnebago...Neenah...our beginnings are kept alive in these names and in the legends left behind by these first inhabitants.

THE LEGEND OF TELULAH
One of the Fox Valley's favorite legends is that of Telulah, a Fox Indian princess. Telulah was the dark-eyed daughter of a Fox chief. Two braves, one of another tribe wanted her as wife and because her father had the power of a leader, he decided the one who could run like the wind would win the princess. The starting point was far up the Fox River, with Telulah waiting for the winner at the largest of several sulphur springs. The chief, wanting the best for his

daughter, told the brave of his own tribe, of a short-cut to the spring. When the brave reached the young girl first, he claimed her as his wife. But Telulah, having stronger feelings for the other runner, was so heartbroken that she sat beside the spring weeping. So often did she shed tears and cry out the name of her true love that the site became known as Telulah's spring, and eventually, Appleton's Telulah Park was named in honor of a beautiful, but sad, Fox Indian princess.

THE LEGEND OF THE PIERCED FOREHEAD
The legend of the pierced forehead was part of the Menominee's oral history that was passed from one generation to the next. It concerned the sturgeon run in the spring of the year. Because the swiftly moving Menominee River met the glistening waters of the great Green Bay, giant sturgeon found their way beyond this mouth to the spawning beds up river. The chief of the village at the first rapids ordered his braves to dam the river with rocks and branches in order to catch the fish by hand. Mountains of fish soon lined

Telulah Park was named after a Fox Indian woman who, legend says, often went to a sulphur spring at the site to weep for her lost lover.

the river banks.

For days the village feasted. They cleaned, smoked and dried the highly-prized white flesh of the sturgeon. Villages up stream counted the days to the sturgeons' coming. Their bellies were hungry and they sent a runner to seek news of the fish. He discovered the dam and the first village's over-abundance of the spring food supply. Days passed and when the dam was not yet broken to release the fish, the chief of the second village sent his son with these words, "Run now to the village of our brother. Tell him our spring has been long and cold, and we are singing songs of hunger while they feast. Ask him to open the dam before the fish swim backward to the big bay."

Because the young boy knew the importance of his mission, he spoke the message again and again inside his head as he ran to the first village. When he gave the message to the chief, there was no reply. The chief grabbed the boy, pinched the skin of his forehead and forced a stone arrowhead through the fold. "Take that as my answer to your father."

The boy returned to his own village. The painful insult in his forehead sent streams of blood down his face. His father's anger was swift and certain. He removed the arrowpoint and his fastest runners carried the bloody stone from village to village. War drums vibrated the trees. Painted braves in long war canoes paddled down river as silently as the hazy smoke of early morning campfires.

They surrounded the first village, and so fierce was their anger that not one member of the tribe was left alive. It became a Menominee legend of revenge and retribution for the holding of the sturgeon and the insult of the pierced forehead.

THE EXPLORERS

Louise Phelps Kellogg, an early research associate of the Wisconsin Historical Society and author of "The French Regime in Wisconsin and the Northwest", suggests "that the Great Lakes, described as an "inland sea", stimulated the imagination of sixteenth-century explorers. Could it be that a great interior lake of which so many rumors had been heard might be the long sought passage to the western ocean?"

It would take another century and the governor of New France, Samuel de Champlain, to solve the mystery of the Great Lakes and their possibility as a route through the continent to the Pacific Ocean and perhaps the Orient. With Champlain the earliest history of Wisconsin begins, and with the first white explorer, legend would give way to recorded history.

The French era of Wisconsin history began with the voyage of Jean Nicolet to the shores of Green Bay in 1634 and ended with the Treaty of Paris of 1763, awarding control over all lands east of the Mississippi River to the British. For 129 years Wisconsin was the outer edge of the French-Canadian tapestry along the St. Lawrence River. Champlain was instrumental in encouraging exploration and promoting the fur trade in the New World. Realizing the importance of domination of the Indians, Champlain sent young Frenchmen to live among them and to learn their languages and customs.

At the invitation of Champlain, Jean Nicolet came to the New World from Cherbourg, the third largest port of France. He was a child of the sea, as were his Viking ancestors, and in this new land he would spend 14 years among the Indians on the upper Ottawa River and then on the eastern shore of Lake Huron. Kellogg described him as "steadfast, adventurous, with a love for the unknown, an excellent memory and an aptitude for languages."

In 1634, 13 years after the Pilgrims landed at Plymouth, the first white man would enter the Fox River Valley. Champlain sent Nicolet on his memorable voyage for two reasons. The Ottawa and the Winnebago were at war and the French fur trade was suffering. Nicolet was to negotiate peace in the interest of lucrative trading. He was also to question the Winnebago as to a possible route to the Pacific. To the French, Winnebago meant "People of the Sea." It was possible they had lived near the salt sea and could provide directions to the Pacific Coast and to the riches of the Orient.

According to historian Reuben Gold Thwaites, Nicolet left Quebec with a large group of fur traders taking on several Huron Indian guides and a birch bark canoe on the way. The small party of eight forged into the wilderness of waterways resting at Sault St. Marie. Heading south, Nicolet's party became the first whites to see Mackinac Island and the great inland sea of Lake Michigan. The expedition followed the Northern shore of this big lake and, finally, glided into "la baie des Puants", the bay of the stinking (salty?) waters—Green Bay.

At the mouth of the Menonimee River, Nicolet made friends with the Menominee Indians who told him he was now near the "people of the sea". The young explorer must have felt a sense of excitement as he sent messengers ahead to announce his arrival. He dressed carefully for these mysterious "orientals" choosing a Chinese robe heavily embroidered with birds and flowers, briliiant with color. Firing pistols from each hand as he stepped ashore, Nicolet sent women and children screaming in fear. This man who carried thunder in his hands was welcomed not by Buddhists and Hindus but by Winnebagos—a tribe of Indians who had lived in this rugged country for centuries before the white man ever knew North America existed. The Winnebago braves were impressed by the white spirit, this manitou of a man. They danced for him and prepared a feast of venison, smoked

The Landfall of Nicolet, a well-known painting by E.W. Deming, depicts the arrival of Jean Nicolet among the Winnebago in 1634. Nicolet's exploration of Lake Michigan, Green Bay, and the Fox Valley opened new areas to the fur trade of New France. SHSW

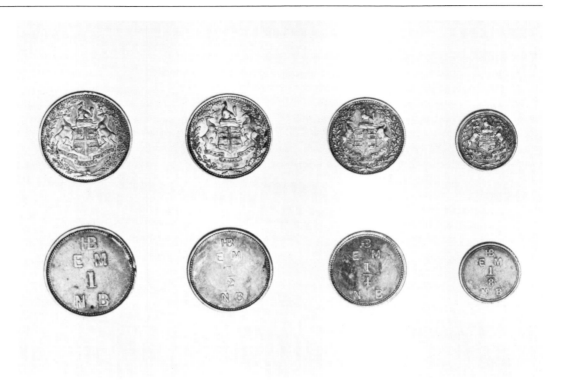

The Hudson's Bay Company's brass tokens once were an important monetary unit in most of the Northwest Territory. They represented one "made" beaver skin—a prime new pelt ready for trade or export—and fractions thereof. SHSW

fish, and 120 beavers.

No one is certain if this historic meeting took place at Green Bay, Red Banks, or on Doty Island but it is clear that Nicolet, later known as the Indian treaty maker, paved the way for the fur traders and missionaries to follow. If the courageous Frenchman failed in his attempt to find a different race of people, his success in dicovering the Great Lakes empire was fair compensation for his journey. It was 20 more years, however, before the coureu du bois and voyageurs braved Nicolet's wilderness trail.

THE FUR TRADERS
In 1654, when an Ottawa trading fleet journeyed to Wisconsin, two young French traders came along; Pierre-Espirit Radisson and Medart Chouart Sieurs de Grosilliers. Radisson and Grosilliers built the first white man's dwelling in Wisconsin, explored much of what is now Wisconsin and Minnesota, and visited the Fox River Valley, opening the door to a century of fur trade.

Because they traded with the Indians without a license, Radisson and Groseilliers were treated as outlaws when they returned to Canada with their furs. Radisson was sent to Paris to answer charges for the illegal trading but later went on to London to help in organizing the Hudson Bay Company. This company would formally establish the rivalry between France and England for the control of the fur trade in the American northwest. The names of the two young and adventurous traders and the story of their days along the Fox might have been lost had it not been for the chance finding of one of Radisson's early journals many years later in the Oxford Library in England.

In the 1660s, following Radisson and Groseilliers came another young Frenchman, Nicolas Perrot. Fur trader, forest diplomat, sometimes called "the greatest Frenchman of the West", Perrot earned the respect and admiration of many Indian tribes. The rapport and alliances he formed with the tribes made him a man to be reckoned with among his fellow fur traders. He was so successful at Indian relations, he even convinced the cantankerous Fox to get along with their neighbors.

In order to protect their fur trade from the English, New France decided to hold a great peace council of all tribes. Perrot was in charge of persuading all of the chiefs to attend the gathering in Sault Ste. Marie where they were to become children of New France. He convinced the Menominee, Sauk, Potawatomi, and Winnebago to accompany him but the Fox, Kickapoo, and Mascoutin refused to go.

The ceremony took place in May, 1671 with a strange assortment of participants.

Fifteen chiefs from different tribes were resplendent in paint and feathers. There were black-robed missionaries, leather-breeched fur traders, and French noblemen in full-dress uniform. Perrot was the interpreter as gifts were exchanged, and Louis XIV was named ruler of Wisconsin.

Perrot received the title of "Commandant of the West" from New France in 1685, and was placed in charge of Green Bay and its surrounding areas, including the upper Mississippi. The extraordinary negotiator left the valley in 1698. Had he stayed, the bloody Fox Wars in the early

This illustration is of Father Joseph Maerst, a Jesuit priest (upper left), and Nicholas Perrot (center) at Fort Saint Antoine. The fort was built by Perrot near Lake Pepin. SHSW

18th century might not have taken place.

THE JESUITS

The coming of the Jesuit missionaries, or "black robes" as the Indians called them, brought the first written history of Wisconsin. These articulate, educated men were not only missionaries, but explorers, map-makers, researchers, and journalists. Each Jesuit was required to write a report of all of his activities and to forward it to his superiors in Quebec as often as possible. Detailed descriptions of Indian tribes, land formation, raging rivers, and life in the wilderness were published annually in a collection called "The Relations". These Jesuit journals are the first official record of life in early Wisconsin.

While colonists struggled to build a new life on a strip of coast along the Atlantic, zealous Frenchmen cut their way to the very heart of the continent and coureurs de bois established a fur trade for the glory of France. Perhaps the men who dreamed the grandest dream of all, however, were the Jesuits who suffered many hardships in their persistent attempts to convert the Indians.

Rene Mehard became the first missionary in Wisconsin when he set up a mission at Chequamegon Bay, called St. Esprit. Menard died in the wilds trying to reach a tribe of Hurons.

Claude Jean Allouez worked the western missions from 1665 until his death in 1689. He reopened St. Esprit and served at least seven different tribes. The work was difficult and discouraging and conversions were few. When he left for the Fox River region in 1669, he was succeeded by Father Jacques Marquette.

Before leaving Wisconsin, Allouez had founded four missions in the Fox River area, including St. Francis Xavier at DePere in 1669, where he ministered to the Potawatomi, Sauk, and eventually the Menominee and Fox. He became known as "the Father of Wisconsin missions" and spent many years learning Indian language and lore in order to become an effective

"man of God." His reports show the work of a sensitive man and a careful observer.

Literally hundreds of Indians were baptized by the Jesuits, but many of them were small children or old people who were near death. William Raney in "Wisconsin, A Story of Progress", attributed the lack of missionary success in Wisconsin to the lessening of French support and fewer recruits to carry on the work. Historian Louise Kellogg suggests that the Indian was proud and independent and was satisfied with his own customs and beliefs. To the Indian the missionary was a mystery. . .someone who made strange signs over dying babies, devoted hours to saying mass and to reading books, and were meek and patient even when assaulted by the Indians.

Fathers Allouez, Marquette, Albanel, André and Silvy were just a few of the courageous Jesuits who carried the Crucifix through Wisconsin in the name of Christianity.

These French missionaries very often accompanied trading expeditions from

Canada to the western Indian tribes. While bootlegging coureurs du bois gathered more and more pelts, control of the fur trade remained firmly in the hands of the Indians. From year to year, Canada's economic fate was measured by the number of furs that reached Montreal.

In the 1670s the French were pushing westward rapidly and fur traders continued to bring news to Quebec of a great river waterway that flowed into a giant sea. Louis Joliet and Father Jacques Marquette, a Jesuit, were chosen to lead an expedition to find the river. In the spring of 1673, with five voyageurs, they set out in two canoes loaded with supplies. They took the now familiar route to Green Bay through the dangerous channel of the upper Fox, and with the help of Mascouten Indian guides, portaged their canoes to the Wisconsin River. The explorers descended the Wisconsin and on June 17, 1673 reached the Mississippi River, the elusive dream of many a French explorer. Reuben Thwaites in "Wisconsin In Three Centuries" recorded Marquette's narrative of the journey. "Catfish struck our canoe with such force that I thought it was a great tree." Thwaits also described paddlefish, sturgeon and wild turkeys. "Though they kept strict watch, they saw no Indians for days and days. Toward evening they would land, build a small fire, cook and eat their supper and sleep in their anchored canoes...all except one, who stood guard."

They continued their journey down the Mississippi, past the mouth of the Missouri, the Ohio, the St. Francis in Arkansas, and spent a night with Arkansas Indians at the mouth of the Arkansas River. With information from the Indians, Joliet and Marquette became convinced that the Mississippi flowed into the Gulf of Mexico and decided not to continue any further less they be captured by Spaniards. Instead they returned to civilization with their new found knowledge. Others may have seen the Mississippi before Joliet and Marquette, but they were the first to travel almost the

length of the mighty river.

They returned to Green Bay by way of the western shore of Lake Michigan. Joliet went on to report in Quebec but lost his maps and journal on the way when his canoe overturned. Father Marquette's journals and maps, completed later at St. Francis Xavier Mission in Green Bay, became the only record of that first

economy. Indians became dependent on the white man's whiskey and credit. Tribes lengthened their hunting seasons. As the importance of the fur trade grew, the power of the Indians expanded. The increasingly wide-ranging search for fur also produced competition and warfare among the tribes. It was a time of transition, conflict, and intense adjustment for the Indians.

The Sauk, the Potawatomi, and, especially, the Fox feared the French control of the Fox-Wisconsin-Mississippi waters. Knowing it could carry trade and arms to their enemy, the Sioux, they worked to prevent the French from crossing Wisconsin in the 1680s. Temporary relief came with the diversion of the war between France and England in 1689 which lessened the local hostilities between the French and the Iroquois. Finally, in 1696 the French decided to close the western posts and to abandon completely their efforts to control fur trade in the region.

At the French withdrawal, Perrot received his orders to leave the Fox River Valley. With Perrot gone, the posts closed, and legalized fur trading prohibited, the Fox tribe were quick to realize their advantage. They demanded payment from any white man who passed through the state and became so troublesome that the government decided on extermination. An expedition of 800 French and Indian allies, led by Louis de Louvigny, was sent to the present site of Neenah and Menasha. The first armed, white force to invade the valley surrounded the Fox village near present-day Little Lake Butte des Morts. The Fox tribe surrendered so that their village might be spared. This same expedition went on to establish the first permanent fort in Wisconsin at Green Bay in 1717.

The Fox convinced the Sauk and Winnebago to unite with their cause and began raids on the Illinois and Chippewa Indians. Secretly aligning themselves with the Sioux, the Fox even threatened to join the Iroquois on the side of the English. These dangerous alliances and the

historic journey. Du Luth, Hennepin, Du Gay, La Salle and many others would follow the trail of Marquette and Joliet making the north-flowing Fox River one of the most important routes into Indian lands.

For nearly 200 years, from 1670 to the mid-1800s, fur trade ruled the land and the lives of its people. The beaver, the muskrat, fox, otter, mink and black bear (all sacred Indian totems) were now traded for kettles, knives, beads, blankets, bracelets, and guns. Beaver skins were the most highly prized and had the greatest influence on the primitive Fox Valley

harassment of local traders caused the French to send another expedition, lead by Constant de Lignery into the valley in 1728. Warned of their coming, the Fox, Sauk and Winnebago retreated westward. Lignery's troops destroyed villages and crops in the hope of starving the Indians during the coming winter. In spite of this, the Fox survived.

Paul Marin, commander of the Green Bay post and known as "the terror", was sent against the Fox in 1729. His troops, disguised as a trading flotilla, paddled up the river to have the unsuspecting Fox shout them ashore. The covering on the boats was thrown off and 150 soldiers opened fire. The Fox retreated to find their village in flames and were again set upon by Marin's men as they sought the protection of the woods. The few pitiful survivors of the Fox tribe gathered their dead and covered them with a mound of earth at the place now known as as Little Lake Butte des Morts or "hill of the dead".

The defeat of the Fox profoundly changed the course of Fox Valley history. If the Fox Indians had not fought to hold the Fox-Wisconsin waterway, other routes might never have developed. If the Fox had been submissive, French rule in the West might never have wavered. The resistance of brave and powerful Fox, dreaded and admired by other tribes, feared and hated by the white man, undermined French influence in the Fox Valley and hurried the forces of change. The Fox Wars ended in 1737 but during the next quarter-century the French would be driven from the valley by another greater power.

Augustin de Langlade had first come to the valley of the Fox as a member of the Lignery expedition. Drawn by the memory of its beauty, he returned to Wisconsin and married the sister of the chief of the Ottawa clan called La Fourche. Because of the lightness of her skin, she was known as "La Blanche", and had much influence with the councils of her tribe. She received Domitelle as a baptismal name. Widow of an early trader she married Augustin in

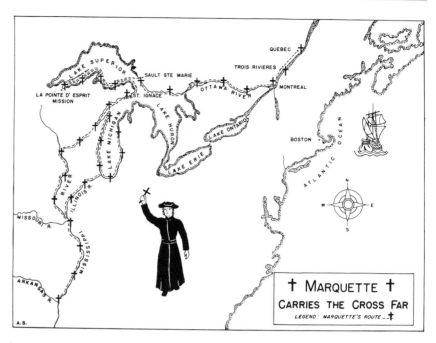

1728. After Domitelle bore their first son, Charles, the Langlade family moved to Green Bay to open a trading business. Augustin, Domitelle, and Charles de Langlade are considered to be the first white settlers of Wisconsin.

Charles de Langlade was proud of his maternal heritage and learned the ways of his Ottawa uncle, Nis-So-Wa-Quet, or as the French called him, La Fourche (The Fork).

His relationship with the powerful Ottawas, his understanding of their language and that of neighboring tribes, and his ability to influence the Indians, convinced the governor of New France to appoint him as commander of French and Indians to fight the English. In 1754 he married Charlotte Bourassa, the daughter of Rene Bourassa, a retired voyageur. Charlotte lived at Mackinac while Charles became renowned for his bravery and carried the Langlade name through many battles in the Seven Years War.

From the end of the French War until the Revolutionary War, Charles de Langlade served the British as superintendent of the Indians and militia in and around Green Bay. According to

In 1916 M.M. Quaife photographed a painting believed to be of Father Jacques Marquette (opposite page). Marquette was an important early explorer of the region and left behind useful documentation of his journeys. His route is illustrated above. SHSW

Moses M. Strong's "History of the Territory of Wisconsin", Charles "received an annuity from the British government of $800, as half pay for his services during the American Revolution."

He died in January, 1800 at the age of 75 and was buried beside his father in a cemetery in Green Bay. His daughter, Domitelle, married Pierre Grignon and had seven sons and two daughters. One of the sons was Augustin Grignon, who would become a familiar name in Fox Valley history.

When the French and Indian War ended with the fall of Quebec and the surrender of Montreal and Canada in the summer of 1760, New France ceased to exist. Throughout the French occupation of Wisconsin and the Fox River Valley, fur was king, and as long as the French and English were rivals, they had to compete for the favor of the Indians.

Wisconsin and the Fox River became part of the British Empire with the signing of the Treaty of Paris in 1763. Throughout the British period and for a long time after, the fur trade continued to flourish. The English paid higher prices for furs, and the Indians became dependent on higher quality goods.

In "Wisconsin, A Story of Progress", historian William Raney credits New Englander Jonathan Carver with the 1766 voyage that resulted in the first description of Wisconsin in the English language.

Because of his experiences in the French and Indian War and his skill as a mapmaker, Carver was a likely candidate to travel the Fox-Wisconsin waterway to the Mississippi, turn northward, cross the continent, and if possible reach the Pacific via a water route. Out of supplies by the time he and his group of travelers reached Lake Superior, they were forced to return to Mackinac. But Carver was a keen observer of the natural beauty of the interior wilderness and wrote of its potential in his journal.

"To what power or authority this new world will become dependent after it has arisen from its present uncultivated state, time alone can discover. There is no doubt that at some future period mighty kingdoms will emerge from these wildernesses, and stately palaces and solemn temples, with gilded spires reaching the skies supplant the Indian huts."

The Wisconsin he described was a virgin wilderness, virtually untouched by French occupation. It was his hope that the English would exert more dominance and take even more advantage of the fur trade.

Carver's book, "Travels in the Interior Parts of North American", was published in 1778, and painted an informative picture of the Fox River Valley in 1766. He told of receiving "the most hospitable and courteous treatment" from all the Indians he encountered. "French settlers who live near the fort in Green Bay cultivate the land and appear to live very comfortably." Around Lake Winnebago the land is reported fertile and "abounding with grapes, plums and other fruit." Where Neenah and Menasha now thrive was the "great town of the Winnebagoes" and their ruler, Glory of the Morning, "a very ancient woman, small in stature."

According to Publius V. Lawson's *History of Winnebago County*, Glory-of-the-Morning was the sister of the head chief of the Winnebago tribe on Doty Island. Her Indian name was Hopokoekau. She married a white man, Sebrevoir DeCarrie, who was an officer in the French army. Glory-of-the-Morning gave birth to three sons and two daughters and would become the mother and grandmother of a noble line of Decorah chiefs.

DeCarrie resigned his commission in 1729, choosing instead to make his living trading with the Winnebago on Doty Island. During the French and Indian War DeCarrie reenlisted in the French army and when he was called to Montreal, Glory-of-the-Morning refused to leave her home and her people. DeCarrie took one of his daughters with him. He was wounded, and he died in a Montreal hospital in 1760.

Glory-of-the-Morning became queen of the Winnebagos and a legend in her own time. An early Neenah-Menasha historian, Mrs. John Kinzie, wrote of the elderly queen in 1831:

No one could tell her age; but all agreed she must have been upwards of 100. Her dimmed eyes were almost white with age, her face darkened and withered like a baked apple, her voice tremulous and feeble, except when raised in fury. She usually went on all fours, not having strength to stand upright.

Henry Merrill, another early historian, described her in 1834:

She was pointed out to me and I was told she must be 143 years old. She lived several years after and was finally burned to death when her wigwam caught fire.

After the Revolutionary War and the establishment of American independence, the population of Wisconsin consisted almost entirely of Indian tribes, small French settlements at Green Bay and Prairie du Chien, and an ever-changing number of English traders.

Niagra, Detroit and Mackinac Island were key posts in the control of western furs, and the Treaty of Paris called for them to be turned over to the Americans. But the British refused to relinquish their dominance over both the Indians and the fur trade. It would take yet another treaty, the Jay Treaty of 1794, to force the transfer of the posts. The fort on Mackinac Island was the last to be turned over in October, 1796. But because the British still traveled freely over the waterways, they continued their control of the fur industry until the War of 1812.

With the triumph of the Americans in the War of 1812 and the Treaty of Ghent in 1814, British rule came to an end in Wisconsin. British soldiers were ordered to evacuate all American territory.

The Americanization of Wisconsin was yet to be accomplished, and for the Fox River Valley the most important consequence of the war was that the United States was in a position to do exactly that.

There were three channels by which goods from Canada were sent into the Mississippi and Missouri country: by way of Chicago and the Illinois River; by Green Bay and the Fox-Wisconsin waterway; and from Lake Superior by way of connecting waterways to the upper Mississippi.

The "great highway" of trade was the Fox-Wisconsin route. Over it were shipped huge quantities of smuggled goods, making their way to the Mississippi without payment of lawful import duties.

The government established military posts at Chicago, Prairie du Chien, and Green Bay to control the illegal traffic. The establishment of Fort Howard at Green Bay and Fort Crawford at Prairie du Chien in the summer of 1816 marks the beginning of army rule in Wisconsin and the valley. Fort Winnebago at the Wisconsin-Fox portage was built 12 years later. The military roads that were carved out of the wilderness to connect the forts west of Lake Michigan were to become Wisconsin's earliest highways. Many of the officers who served in these rugged frontier posts went on to etch their name in American history....Zachary Taylor, Jefferson Davis, and Civil War general Edmund Kirby Smith were but a few.

In the 182 years since Nicolet had left his footprints on the shores of Green Bay, civilization in the valley of the Fox had seen little change. The nationality of the traders had shifted from French to British to American but fur trade was still the dominant force in valley life. The next decades would bring profound changes as the land revealed new sources of opportunity. A new era of American trading, farming, and industrialization was about to begin.

The Passage

For a century and a half the history of the Fox River Valley had been carved by Indians, explorers, and fur traders. White settlements along the river had been sporadic and temporary. Only the bravest of the early pioneers had discovered the lush valley and few had stayed. It took the possibility of quick riches in the lead region of southeastern Wisconsin to attract the first wave of permanent settlers.

In 1827, the Fox-Wisconsin rivers were protected by bookend forts Green Bay in the east and Prairie

Right
Hendrick Aupaumut, known more commonly as Captain Hendrick, enlisted in the American army in 1775, where he received a captain's sword from General George Washington. In 1792 he was sent by Secretary of War Henry Knox on a peace mission to the Western Indians. He spoke, along with Menominee Chief Tomah, against joining Tecumseh's Pan-Indian rebellion. Captain Hendrick also served under General William Henry Harrison in the War of 1812. He was instrumental in bringing the Stockbridge tribe of the Mohawk Nation to settle in the Fox Valley, where he died in 1830. He is one of two Revolutionary War veterans, both Stockbridge Indians, buried in Kaukauna. SHSW

Previous page
The prehistoric burial mound the "Hill of the Dead" gave Butte des Morts its name. The actual Hill of the Dead was probably constructed in prehistoric times by Woodland Indians. In about 1750 Butte des Morts had been the scene of a final battle in which a French-Indian alliance drove the Fox Indians from the valley, and in 1827 it served as the location for concluding a treaty with the Chippewa Indians. The site was destroyed during construction of a railroad bridge at present Fritse Park on the west shore of Little Lake Butte des Morts. From J.O. Lewis, The Aboriginal Portfolio, 1835. SHSW

du Chien as the westernmost outpost where the Wisconsin River entered the Mississippi. Between the two strongholds snaked 300 miles of winding rivers and lakes—wilderness sacred to the Winnebago tribe. It would take the Winnebago War of 1827 and the Black Hawk War of 1832 to convince the white

people of southern Wisconsin that the Indians should be pushed beyond the Mississippi River.

As white fortune hunters and pioneers moved in to mine the valuable lead, they trespassed further and further on Winnebago land. When word reached the tribe that two of their warriors had been

imprisoned and killed for stealing, they had no way of knowing it was only a rumor. The Winnebago tribal code demanded two enemy scalps for that of one Indian. The duty to wreak vengeance fell upon Red Bird, a Winnebago Chief whose father had earlier been cheated out of his land by white men. Red Bird chose two of his finest braves, We-Kau and Chickhonsik, and went to the cabin of Registre Gagnier, a half-breed farmer. Because of his friendship with the Indians, Gagnier invited them inside to share food and tobacco. Revenge came swiftly as the raiders shot the farmer and his hired man and took their scalps and that of Gagnier's

young daughter, whom they had stabbed to death. Gagnier's wife escaped with their 10-year old son to neighbors who quickly spread the alarm.

Red Bird and his men joined a hunting party of Winnebago warriors. This band fired at two keel boats on the Wisconsin River, killing several men. The new attack coupled with the Gagnier deaths, panicked the white settlers into believing it was a full-fledged Indian uprising.

Wisconsin's Governor Cass called in all available troops. Full regiments rushed up the Wisconsin River to join forces with soldiers coming up the Fox. The combined force set up camp to wait for more troops.

Red Bird Surrendering to Major William Whistler near Portage, Wisconsin, September 1, 1827, a painting by Hugo Ballin, hangs in the Governor's reception room of the Wisconsin capitol. SHSW

The statue of Red Bird at High Cliff overlooks Lake Winnebago. SHSW

From their vantage point on the bluff overlooking Portage they could keep watch to the north and south. But there was no need for reinforcements as a Winnebago runner brought the message from Red Bird and the fugitives that they would surrender before another sun could set.

Soldiers lined up in full-dress uniform as 30 Indians emerged from the forest with Red Bird in the lead carrying the white flag of truce. It was a dramatic moment as the six-foot chief, dressed in white elkskin, approached his enemies. The war pipe of his people was laced over his heart and in man's justice would spare his brothers. Red Bird's plea was ignored as he was chained and imprisoned until he could be tried. President Andrew Jackson eventually pardoned Red Bird—but too late. The once proud Winnebago chief died in prison. His carefully wrapped body was returned to the valley to rest in his ancestral burial grounds.

The spirit of Chief Red Bird has been carved in a statue at High Cliff State Park overlooking the land of the Winnebago. It still is said that when the sunset colors the sky over the lake and the wind is just

The Ducharme-Grignon cabin in Kaukauna was rendered in pen and ink by Mary Mergy in 1982. The original portion on the left was built by Dominique Ducharme in 1790; the right portion was added by Augustine Grignon in 1818. The cabin fell into ruin in the late 1800s.

one hand he carried the pipe of peace. Facing the commanding officer he chanted his own death song in a voice strong and full:

> *"I am ready, but I do not want to be put in irons.*
> *Let me be free.*
> *I have given my life.*
> *I would not take it back.*
> *It is gone."*

Asking for death, he hoped the white

right, Red Bird's death song can be heard.

THE EARLY SETTLERS

Dominique Ducharme is credited with being the first white settler in the Fox River Valley. Born in Lachine, Quebec, Canada in 1763, Ducharme followed his father's occupation of fur trading in Wisconsin. He married Susan Larose, daughter of a French trader, in Green Bay and moved his trading to Grand Kakalin (Kaukauna) in the early 1790s, according to historian Lambert MaCabey.

Augustine Grignon was the first man of European ancestry born in present-day Wisconsin. The last of the French-Canadian fur traders in the Fox Valley, Grignon became the first person to use the water power of the Fox for purposes of industry and commerce. SHSW

of the portage. Before the deal was final, Ducharme had had to throw in one more barrel of rum.

Dominique Ducharme built a trading post, house, barn and a number of outbuildings on his property before leaving Kaukauna to take over his father's estate in Canada. He sold his Wisconsin land and holdings to his brother Paul, a bachelor. Paul Ducharme continued the trading post until 1813, when part of the land was sold to Augustin Grignon. Ducharme built another home and store on the upper part of the remaining property, farmed the land, and portaged the river for travelers. When the Stockbridge and Brothertown Indians were moved from New York state to Wisconsin in the early 1820s, they lived on land secured from the Menominee near Kaukauna. In 1834 they were moved to Calumet County. The loss of Indian trade at his store and the general decline of the fur industry caused financial difficulties for Paul Ducharme. He borrowed money from Judge John Lawe of Green Bay and in 1836 Paul deeded his property to Lawe as payment of his debts.

The Grignon brothers were also important in the white settlement of the Fox Valley. Born in Green Bay, Augustin and Hippolyte were sons of Green Bay fur trader, Pierre Grignon, and grandsons of Charles de Langlade. Augustin early learned to appreciate the land and people as he traveled throughout the valley on his trading missions. Near Kaukauna, he met and married Nancy McCrea, the daughter of a Scottish fur trader and a Menominee woman. Augustin and Nancy Grignon bought the Ducharme land in 1813 and enlarged the original cabin, adding a trading post. They began to cultivate the land and raise a family along with their crops. It was here that Charles, Alexander, Paul, Louis, Margaret, and Sophia Grignon were born. For many years the Grignon cabin was the only house on the river from Fort Howard at Green Bay to Fort Winnebago at Portage.

The valley's first real entrepreneur, Augustin Grignon not only did a brisk

In 1793 Ducharme bought all of present-day Kaukauna from the Indians for two barrels of rum. The land deed was signed by Ducharme and two Menominee, Wabispine and Tobacnoir. Ducharme signed his name and the Indians signed with drawings of an eagle and a duck. This document became one of the oldest recorded land deeds in Wisconsin. Ducharme's ownership was not readily accepted by all of the Indians in the area. Mes (the Eagle) and Bitte (the Beaver) visited the trader to claim ownership of the same land and demand their share of the payment. Ducharme paid five more barrels of rum and an extra barrel for their share business at his trading post, but became a mill owner in 1816. His saw mill was the first in the area to be powered by water. The unruly Fox River provided yet another profitable venture in the portaging of travelers' goods around the rapids. Over the years, as the Grignons' fortune grew, their home was expanded and improved. The house with its white-pillared porch came to be known as "the mansion in the woods". Once it stood alone as a sentinel for the wild and noisy river, surrounded

of their territory with a treaty that released lands east of the waters of Green Bay, Lake Winnebago and the Milwaukee River, and were taught the arts of civilization by their white brothers. Acreage was cleared, log houses and a mill were built on the island of Winnebago Rapids, now a part of Neenah and Menasha. The Indian men were taught to farm and make timber and the women learned household duties.

The Indians, however, did not like the uncomfortable, wooden houses and tore up

by peaceful meadows and woods. Today, it stands as a majestic reminder of the ever-changing life along the Fox.

The Fox River snaked its way through the Menominee Indians' ancestral lands and was a vital link in the water route from the Great Lakes to the Mississippi. The white settlers wanted control and during the 12 years in which Wisconsin was a territory the Indians were out-maneuvered into giving up most of their land. The Menominee had already relinquished a small tract of Fox River land to the New York Indians. In 1831 the Menominee were pushed into the interior

the plank flooring to build fires. The white man's ways were strange to the Menominee, who found it more sensible to pitch teepees outside and shelter their horses inside the drafty log cabins.

THE TREATY OF CEDARS

In 1836, at a place called "The Cedars" near Little Chute and across the river from where Kimberly now stands, a treaty was signed relinquishing Indian ownership of the Fox River Valley. The Treaty of Cedars gave four million acres of land to the United States government for $692,110 in cash and provisions to the Menominee.

Opposite page, top
The Winnebago Indians inhabited the Fox Valley area when the French explorers arrived. These Winnebago women wore full tribal dress when they were photographed in 1910. SHSW

Opposite page, bottom
A state marker commemorates the signing of the Treaty of the Cedars, on the riverbank near today's Highway 96 just west of Little Chute. From the Mackesy Collection of the Outagamie County Historical Society, Inc. (OCHS)

Henry Dodge, governor of Wisconsin, explained that he had been sent by the Great Father in Washington to buy the land located between the Fox and the Wolf as far north as the Menominee River. "It is not the value of your country", Dodge said, "but the future and lasting happiness and the great regard the Great Father has for his red children that has caused this proposition to be made to you."

Chiefs Oshkosh, A-Yam-A-Taw, Big Wave, Little Wave, Shaw-We-Naw, and their people took six days to consider the treaty and finally Chief Oshkosh spoke:

"Our Great Father has made up his mind to get a piece of our land. I have consulted my nation and we have made up our minds to let you have the land we have marked upon the map."

The Indians had marked an area that lay between the Wolf River and Green Bay and ran northward into upper Michigan as the piece to be sold to the Great Father. For this they asked $1,950,820 plus tobacco, salt, and other provisions with an additional $186,420 to pay off debts to traders.

Governor Dodge responded with a final offer of the original $692,110 (with $20,000 to be used for educational purposes). Chief Oshkosh accepted Dodge's offer and said:

"My chiefs and nation are satisfied with the offer you have made us, and they have told us it was a good price for our lands, and we find everything as you mentioned to us in council. We agree to accept it. There is only one thing we do not like in this treaty, that is the money for a school. We do not want schools, we do not wish our children to read papers. We are willing to accept the amount to our friend and relation, Robert Grignon. We wish him to receive one thousand dollars every year for 20 years. I am satisfied and all my nation is satisfied. We are glad to shake your hand in friendship."

With the signing of the Treaty of Cedars on September 3, 1836, the entire Fox River Valley was opened to the white man.

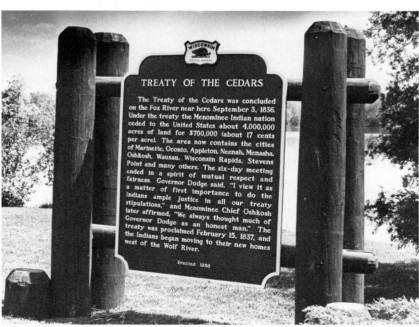

TREATY OF THE CEDARS

The Treaty of the Cedars was concluded on the Fox River near here September 3, 1836. Under the treaty the Menominee Indian nation ceded to the United States about 4,000,000 acres of land for $700,000 (about 17 cents per acre). The area now contains the cities of Marinette, Oconto, Appleton, Neenah, Menasha, Oshkosh, Wausau, Wisconsin Rapids, Stevens Point and many others. The six-day meeting ended in a spirit of mutual respect and fairness. Governor Dodge said, "I view it as a matter of first importance to do the Indians ample justice in all our treaty stipulations," and Menominee Chief Oshkosh later affirmed, "We always thought much of Governor Dodge as an honest man." The treaty was proclaimed February 15, 1837, and the Indians began moving to their new homes west of the Wolf River.

Erected 1958

been modernized, updated and added to. The steeple can be seen for miles throughout the Fox River Valley, from Appleton, from Kimberly, and from busy Highway 41. In the darkness it is a lighted sentinel, glowing perhaps with a bit of mystery, reminding us of our passage from one century to another.

KAUKAUNA

Probably no other city in the Fox Valley has had as many names as Kaukauna. It is believed to have originated from the Menominee word, "Ogaq-Kane" (the place of the pike), or "O-Gau-Gau-Ning" (the eddies where the fish stop). The Indian names were distorted by French usage and became Cacalin, Kakalin, Kockaloc, cacolin, and Kaukaulin until the official change to Kaukauna by the state legislature in 1851.

Known by early settlers as "the lion of

Above
The Vanden Berg homestead is portrayed circa 1850. It is on present-day Depot Street in Little Chute. From the Van Handel Collection, OCHS

Left
In 1948 Little Chute residents celebrated the village centennial.

the Fox", Kaukauna is the oldest settlement in Outagamie County. In 1816 Kaukauna had the first grist mill in the state to be operated by water power, and a water-operated saw mill soon followed. Business in the little settlement continued to grow as the Stockbridge and other

eastern Indians settled on the south side of the river in 1822. The Indians were a good market for the products of Kaukauna mills and stores until 1834 when they moved to their own settlement.

When the Treaty of the Cedars was signed in 1836, a land rush started in the

An otherwise placid scene is punctuated by the white water of the Kaukauna rapids, photographed circa 1890.

Fox River Valley. As quickly as the land could be surveyed, settlers staked their claims and bought through the land office at Green Bay. French Canadians, Dutch, Irish, and Germans were settling on farmlands in an ever-widening ripple.

Morgan L. Martin, a New Yorker who came to Wisconsin in 1827, gave both effort and money to the improvement of the Fox and Wisconsin rivers. In 1846 Congress made land along the river available for $1.25 an acre and proposed an extensive canal project for the Fox. The first attempt of the United States government to improve the Fox River for navigational purposes is recorded in the congressional act of August 8, 1846, providing for a grant of land to the State of Wisconsin for which the state was to make improvements on the waterway. In 1848 it was turned over to a state board of public works, with C.R. Alton as chief engineer.

In 1851 the state agreed that Martin would continue work on the waterway, using his own resources. He was to be reimbursed from the sale of land grants. He hired 500 men, and in 1853 the Fox and Wisconsin Improvement Company was organized. Martin named himself president and enlisted the aid of a number of Wisconsin capitalists. By 1855, the locks were almost completed, but land sales could not keep pace with construction costs, and investors had already spent $400,000. Money was acquired from eastern capitalists to complete the project, and for several years the lower Fox and Lake Winnebago were filled with river traffic. The completion of the canals triggered another building boom and the number of houses and stores rapidly multiplied.

When George Lawe platted Kaukauna in 1851, the rival city of Springville was laid out and recorded just across the river. Springville was the transfer point

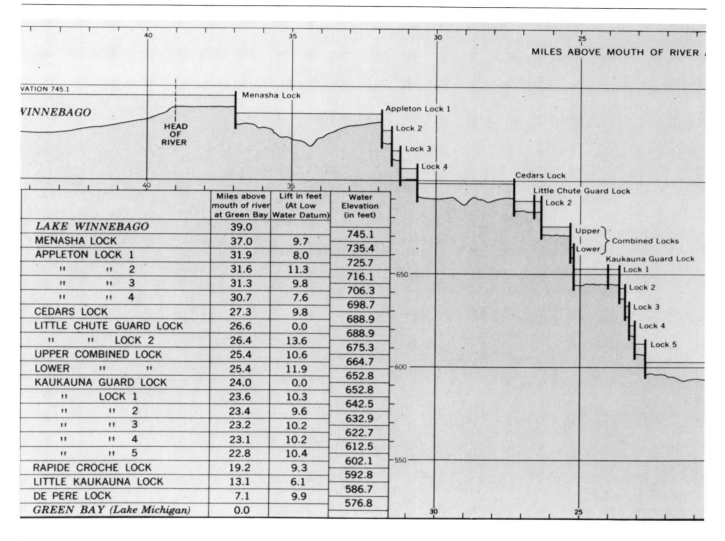

	Miles above mouth of river at Green Bay	Lift in feet (At Low Water Datum)	Water Elevation (in feet)
LAKE WINNEBAGO	39.0		
MENASHA LOCK	37.0	9.7	745.1
APPLETON LOCK 1	31.9	8.0	735.4
" " 2	31.6	11.3	725.7
" " 3	31.3	9.8	716.1
" " 4	30.7	7.6	706.3
CEDARS LOCK	27.3	9.8	698.7
LITTLE CHUTE GUARD LOCK	26.6	0.0	688.9
" " LOCK 2	26.4	13.6	688.9
UPPER COMBINED LOCK	25.4	10.6	675.3
LOWER " "	25.4	11.9	664.7
KAUKAUNA GUARD LOCK	24.0	0.0	652.8
" LOCK 1	23.6	10.3	652.8
" " 2	23.4	9.6	642.5
" " 3	23.2	10.2	632.9
" " 4	23.1	10.2	622.7
" " 5	22.8	10.4	612.5
RAPIDE CROCHE LOCK	19.2	9.3	602.1
LITTLE KAUKAUNA LOCK	13.1	6.1	592.8
DE PERE LOCK	7.1	9.9	586.7
GREEN BAY (Lake Michigan)	0.0		576.8

from boat to horse and wagon for hauling merchandise from Green Bay to Neenah. But Springville never really prospered and could not compete with the bustling town of canal workers across the river.

Most of the workers left Kaukauna when the river work was completed and many of the empty buildings in the village were sold to local farmers. The next winter these structures were skidded across the snow to be used for rural barns and homes, making an eerie end to this early building boom.

Kaukauna slept through the early 1860s, but awoke with a start with the arrival of the Chicago and Northwestern Railroad.

Factories and mills sprang up overnight. By 1870 Kaukauna citizens were working at the Nichols and Company Stave Factory, the Stovekin Grist Mill run by John Stovekin, the Diedrich Sawmill, and the Reuter Spoke Factory. John Stovekin built the town's first paper mill in 1873 and in less than two years it was producing three tons of straw paper a day.

Kaukauna once again had a rival with the establishment of Ledyard. When the Milwaukee Lake Shore and Western Railway built their shops on the south side of the river, the Kaukauna Water Power Company also bought land there, built a canal, and platted the village of

The Lower Fox River falls 168.3 feet from Lake Winnebago to Green Bay. This detail from a government nautical chart shows a cross-section of the tremendous drop of the river from Menasha through Kaukauna. Although the river posed a considerable challenge to pioneer boatmen, its water-power potential was obvious to the first French and Yankee settlers. Courtesy, National Oceanic and Atmospheric Administration, United States Department of Commerce

Right
George W. Lawe, representative of the last of the British-American fur traders in the Fox Valley, is known as the "Father of Kaukauna." Lawe supervised the first Kaukauna Town Plat in 1851, built roads with the help of Menominee Indians, and constructed the first bridge across the Fox River at Kaukauna in 1851.

Far right
H.A. Frambach came to Kaukauna—after serving brilliantly in the Civil War—to develop flour and paper mills with John Stovekin. Frambach became president of the Kaukauna Electric Light Company in 1884. In 1885 he organized the precursor of the Bank of Kaukauna and became the city's first mayor. Much of the political, commercial, industrial and cultural progress of Kaukauna during the late 1800s may be attributed to Colonel Frambach's leadership.

Ledyard.

Within four years the population of Ledyard zoomed to 934, and in 1884 the village petitioned for a charter. Officers were elected and a city seal adopted, but incorporation never came. Residents on both sides of the Fox River favored a common city of Kaukauna and Ledyard. On March 25, 1885, the two villages became one by an act of the Wisconsin Legislature.

The 1880s and 90s saw years of progress with the Meade-Edward Waterpower Project and the building of the Hewitt Canal. Paper mills flourished because of developments in power, and jobs were plentiful at the Badger Paper Company, the Outagamie Mill, Krause Fibre Mill, Ruse Paper and the Shartle Paper Company.

At the time that German-born Oscar Thilmany joined forces with Jacob and Robert Nunnemacher, John LeLones and W.A. Doane to start the American Pulp Company, the paper-making industry was just beginning in the Fox River Valley and northeastern Wisconsin. The company, located in the old Otis and Doane Fibre Mill, opened its doors on September 18, 1883, The mill's first workforce, ten men and eight women, produced six tons of pulp per day. In 1889 Oscar Thilmany moved from Appleton to Kaukauna to live in a house overlooking the mill, and became sole owner of the newly named Thilmany Pulp and Paper Company that survives to this day.

Electric lights, a community newspaper, dreams of great wealth from the discovery of gas wells and coal beds, the founding of churches and schools, a police department, Driving Park Association with its famous horseraces, paddle-wheel excursions up the Fox River: all had a part in the long and colorful history of Kaukauna.

COMBINED LOCKS
Roland Garner built his farm on a hill overlooking the Fox river in the 1830s and it became Garner's Landing. Many years

Left
German gemütlichkeit *joined with the natural beauty of Eden Park in Kaukauna a century ago. Natural wood footbridges led excursionists from a steamboat landing on the Fox River to a delightfully landscaped German* biergarten, *which featured dancing and feasting for the entire family.*

Below
The Badger Paper Mill of Kaukauna featured innovations of the most modern factory of its day. It contained six grinders (invented by Colonel H.A. Frambach to make wood pulp) steam heat, electricity, and a fire engine in the basement with water hoses running to all the floors. Despite the built-in fire-fighting equipment, the Badger mill followed two earlier Frambach mills to a smoldering demise in the early 1900s.

The arrival of the railroad meant economic prosperity for many towns throughout the United States in the 1800s. This is suggested in an illustration of a locomotive alongside the Appleton Pulp and Paper Company mill (right). The Milwaukee Lake Shore and Western Railway moved its division headquarters to Ledyard (now south Kaukauna) in 1881, bringing 200 employees with their families. The subsequent boom turned the sleepy flag station of Ledyard into a major commercial center in the area. A scene of south Kaukauna (below right) shows the growth that the town experienced.

Above
Members of the Lawrence University athletic team posed for a photograph in 1893.

Left
The Lawrence Bicycle Club gathers at Ormsby Hall, the first women's dormitory, in 1894. From the Mackesy Collection, OCHS

Lawrence's first photography class sits on the steps of Science Hall in 1900.

Reeder Smith's family arrived in Appleton in 1849. A year earlier the John F. Johnstons, who were married in Neenah, moved into their shanty and became the first permanent residents of Appleton. Mrs. J.S. Buck, the second white woman to arrive, described the Johhston house as "a haven, a first home for all settlers, it being also a hotel, hospital, tavern, post office, town hall and church."

When more settlers came, three competitive settlements sprang up: Appleton, Lawesburg to the east, and Grand Chute to the west. Shanties bordered the river bank and Reeder Smith, who was in charge of laying out the city, wrote to Amos Lawrence; "I am greatly surprised to find such determination to

Left
Irish and German work gangs built the canals and dams which would become important to the growth of Appleton.

Below left
The upper dam at Appleton was built near present-day Memorial Drive Bridge.

statehood in 1848 brought another wave of immigrants into the valley and shanties sprang up faster than Elder Sampson, Reeder Smith, Hoel Wright and Colonel Henry Blood could lay out plots. Colonel Blood supervised new roads and opened a stage coach line and a store. The Appleton post office was established in 1849 with John F. Johnston as first postmaster, and the first consignment of mail—four newspapers and one letter—was brought from Green Bay. W.S. Warner set up the first dry goods store, and the industrial development of the city was born when C.R. Riggs built the first saw mill for Amos Lawrence in 1848.

Improvement of the river started in 1850, and a $200 bridge spanned the Fox and remained for two years as the only way of crossing except by boat. When the census was taken that year there were 619 people, and Daniel Huntley opened the first free public school for 60 students. His salary was $28 a month and he paid for his own board.

In 1853, when the village of Appleton was incorporated and John F. Johnston was named village president, the *Crescent,* the city's first newspaper was founded by Samuel Ryan, Jr. Appleton was then described as having a "salubrious climate, enchanting scenery, delightful drives and beautiful surroundings". Some even claimed that the water from Telulah spring had health giving gualities. The growth of the valley's pioneer economy was directly related to the development of water power and a navigable transportation network. The Fox, which flows north into Green Bay, is divided into two distinct sections by Lake Winnebago. The upper section, from Portage to Lake Winnebago, is 107 miles long and has a fall of almost 40 feet. The lower section, from the lake to De Pere, is 31 miles long and falls 166 feet.

The United States goverment began efforts to improve the Fox River in 1846, and two years later granted improvement rights to the state of Wisconsin. The state board of public works made plans for canals with a bottom width of 40 feet and a four-foot depth, 125-foot locks that would measure 30 feet in width, and with wing dams on the Wisconsin river. Irish and German work gangs supplied manual labor. In 1850 and 51, dams were built across both the Neenah and Menasha natural outlets of the lake.

In 1853 the state turned over further improvement of the river to the Fox and Wisconsin Improvement Company, a private corporation that wanted to enlarge the locks to 160 feet and 35 feet wide, with a five foot depth. In 1856 the improvement work was sold by the state to the Green Bay and Mississippi Canal Company. In 1872 the United States paid the company $145,000 and took charge of all navigational work. Their plan of attack was four-pronged: the repair and replacing of existing works on the Fox; the construction of additional locks and dams to complete the system of slackwater navigation on the upper river; the deepening and widening of the channels; the completion of the improvement of the Wisconsin River; and finally, the replacement of all the existing locks and dams with permanent fixtures.

Meanwhile Appleton was coming to depend more and more on its water power. The first paper mill was built by the Richmond Brothers in 1853 and was regarded as a "risky, dare-devil type operation" by a cautious editor of the time. The following year 14 industries depended on the river as a source of power. In the few years between village and city incorporation, growth and progress was nothing short of phenomenal.

River navigation was still a problem and the Fox proved to be a barrier as well as a water roadway. In 1849, when the *Snowbird* came up the Fox River as far as Kaukauna, it had to be hauled out of the water, placed on skids, transferred to Appleton, relaunched, and sailed to Oshkosh. With the success of the Erie Canal as an example, a Fox canal seemed to be the answer for getting products and supplies to and from market.

The first boats to navigate the Fox River, other than the canoes of Indians and explorers, were old Durham scows. Earlier fur traders depended on the bateau, which was propelled by small poles, a crew of a dozen men, and could carry ten to twelve tons of freight. With the Americans came the Durham, named for its Pennsylvania inventor. It was usually forty to sixty feet long, ten to twelve feet wide, carried twenty to thirty tons, and drew eighteen inches of water. They were awkward and cumbersome and it took a great deal of time and effort to move them with the help of long poles and oxen. The oxen had to be driven through shallow water as they pulled the heavy boats for many miles up and down the river. The Durham boat was introduced to Wisconsin by John P. Arndt, who began building them at Green Bay in 1825. Within just a few years they outnumbered all other craft on the Fox and Wisconsin until the advent of the steamboat.

After the government started work on the river, large sternwheelers churned the waters between Green Bay and Oshkosh. *The Evelyn...Leander Choate...The Paul Fox...Wolf...The Thistle...B.F. Carter* and the *J.H. Marston* provided excursions on the river and Lake Winnebago. Some also hauled marsh hay, limestone and brick.

River improvement progressed and in 1856 the steamboat *Aquila* tooted its horn to the cheering river-front crowds in Appleton as it passed by on its first complete trip from Milwaukee to Green Bay. By the next year a wave of river traffic brought 24 steamers a week to the busy little port of Appleton.

For the tidy sum of $2,000, an enterprising man could get into the steamboat business by buying or building a boat and contracting for cargo or passengers, or both. The boats ran from Green Bay to Kaukauna, and Appleton to Oshkosh. Passengers could pass through as many as 17 locks and 56 miles of "the most beautiful scenery in Wisconsin". Tea, coffee and light meals were served, or passengers could bring a picnic lunch. With the laughter, singing and clapping in time to the music of local bands, the trip quickly

passed as a "jolly time" was had by all.

Canoes, French-Canadian bateaux, pole-pushed Durham boats, steamers, industrial barges: each was married to the river in its time. But the success of the canal turned out to be short-lived, for the railroad was to replace it as the iron link to Wisonsin's developing markets.

KING PINE
In the early and mid-1800s, stately white pines covered the land in the Fox River Valley as far as the eye could see. Wisconsin was part of a giant forest belt that stretched from New England through

In 1849 William Smith Warner paid $50 apiece for the first four lots ever sold in Appleton. As overseer of roads, in 1850 he helped to clear timber to create College Avenue. He was a merchant for several years until he could afford to set up a law practice, which flourished for more than 30 years. Warner held a variety of city offices in both Kaukauna and Appleton, and served in the Wisconsin legislature in 1877.

Above
The Evelyn, *shown passing through the lock at Little Chute, was built in 1883. It was unusually long, 143 feet, and carried both passengers and freight. From the Mackesy Collection, OCHS*

Right
The steamers Fox *and* Wolf *take a rest from their canal-dredging work and winter at the first Appleton lock in 1910.*

The family and friends of Fox Valley entrepreneur John Stevens traveled the Fox River, Lake Winnebago, and the Great Lakes on the steam yacht Cambria.

the Great Lakes and dominated the northern three-fifths of the state. "King white pine" thrived in the north country along Lake Michigan and along all of the major rivers, including the Fox, Oconto, Menominee, Pestigo, Wisconsin, and Wolf.

Cities, sprouting across Wisconsin and adjoining states, demanded lumber. Fast-growing Chicago and Milwaukee needed huge volumes. Prairie states looked with envy to the white pine of Wisconsin. Orders came from everywhere, and the white pine, some as old as 400 years and reaching heights of 180 to 250 feet, was the mother lode of the forest. Its wood was extremely strong for its light weight. It was slow to decay and easy to work, dried without warping and was not affected by weather or time—a perfect choice for building and pattern-making.

The Wolf River, which joins the Fox a few miles west of Oshkosh, flowed through some of the best of Wisconsin's white pine. In 1854 the Wolf River Basin provided the logs for 40 million board feet of lumber, and peak production came 20 years later with 205 million board feet and over 80 lumber camps.

Lumbering's influence on the development of Wisconsin and the Fox River Valley was striking. Green Bay's location at the mouth of the Fox River on the bay made it a major supply and export center for the hustling lumber industry. The state's first saw mill was built near Green Bay in 1809 and another was built in 1812. Saw mills were built in Oshkosh as early as 1847 and soon it was called "Sawdust City". Appleton, Neenah and Menasha processed logs from their own surroundings as well as the Wolf River. Lumbering influenced the growth of many of these Wisconsin villages and cities and would eventually influence railroad companies in deciding rail routes.

In spite of the lesson to be learned from Wisconsin's depleted fur supply, the land was still looked upon as a bottomless reservoir of raw materials and resources. By 1890, except for choice timber that still remained on the Menominee Indian Reservation, the virgin pine was gone.

WHEAT
Wheat—the cash crop, the golden grain that dominated life in the valley for a

A. Syme's flouring mills operated in Menasha during the late 1800s.

decade—adapted well to the needs of pioneer farmers. It could be planted with little soil preparation and virtually ignored until harvest time. Wheat stored well and commanded as much as $1.18 to $1.25 per bushel in 1859. Flour was $6 and $7 a barrel. The one great disadvantage of wheat was the need for a rapid harvest. Wheat ripens quickly and must be cut and gathered before it begins to shatter. Harvesting was a tedious procedure using a hand scythe followed by gathering and binding by hand. Once harvested it could be stored in the shock, threshed, cleaned and hauled later.

Flour and grist mills grew up along the Fox River almost as quickly as the wheat itself. In the late 1850s and early 1860s, before the grain fields swept westward, Wisconsin was the leading wheat-producing state, and more wheat was raised than all other crops combined. For a short time, the Fox River Valley was recognized as the grain center of the mid-west.

Oftentimes farmers had to travel 20 and 30 miles from field to mill. A full load of 25 bushels of wheat weighed about 1,500 pounds, an exhausting load for a team on roads which were only wilderness paths in many areas. After the harvest it was common to see a caravan of teams (as many as 100 a day) hauling wheat over the plank road between Menasha and Kaukauna. The streets of Menasha were lined with teams, their owners spending the night in their wagons or in the mills waiting their turn for grinding. At the mills wrought iron wall lanterns burned all night long for days on end as the mill wheels kept grinding.

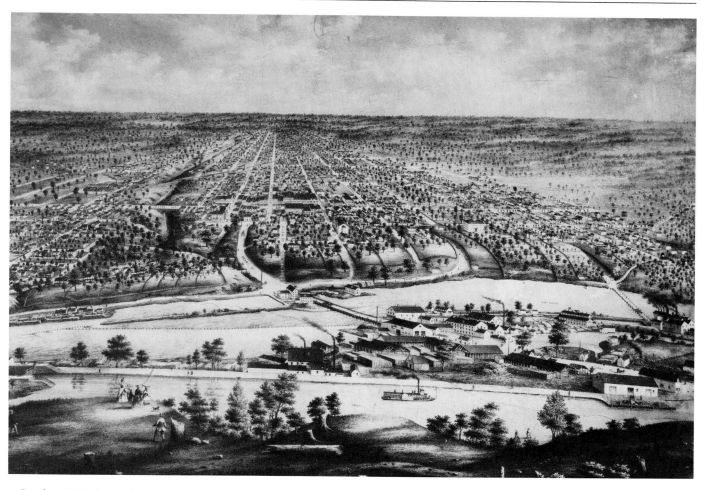

In the 1860s large flour mills on the river front were doing a $1,000,000-a-year business as long as the abundance poured from fertile fields. Some of the early settlers who came to the twin cities were millers and millwrights. Their skilled labor helped put Neenah-Menasha in control of the local flour market. Surpluses were shipped to outside markets via the Lower Fox to Green Bay. Neenah's six mills and Menasha's two, were producing 50,000 barrels of flour by 1860 and they were ranked as the second largest flour producer in the state, second only to Milwaukee. By 1870 Neenah had eleven mills and Menasha had three. They put out 233,850 barrels of flour that year.

But the soil could not sustain so many years of grain cropping and production dropped. Farmers grew winter wheat

because of its higher yield of premium flour, but too often freezing weather came early and bit deeply with its winter kill. Chinch bugs, smut and rust took their toll and winter wheat began to move west.

As wheat farming moved farther West, flour-milling could not continue to be the giant industry supporting the two thriving cities. Minneapolis, 300 miles away, had railroads that opened to the new wheat lands to the west and the rapid growth of Minneapolis flour milling in the 1870s, destroyed Neenah and Menasha's aspirations. But the disappointment would only prove that the cities' business leaders were flexible, that they could focus in a new direction. Flour milling would soon be forgotten as local entrepreneurs looked with enthusiasm to a promising, new kind of manufacturing.....papermaking.

The growth of Appleton in both transportation and waterpower is illustrated in this 1874 bird's-eye view. Wood products and flour eventually gave way to pulp, paper, and the manufacturing of machinery.

Patterns of Life

The patterns of life in the Fox Cities changed profoundly in the mid-19th century. Small frontier communities of rough-hewn log buildings and the roads foot deep in mud grew in an astonishingly short period of time into cities with clapboard houses, streetcars, and cultural societies. The Fox River and its tributaries would no longer serve as a path but as a source of power drawing a flood of immigrants in search of opportunity.

In 1851, Samuel Freeman described Appleton in these words:

There are some nine or ten mercantile establishments at this place, the most of which would class respectably with those of older towns. Appleton has three public houses of commodious size, some of which are noted for their excellence; and Lawesburgh, one of mammoth dimensions, just about to commence business. In short, there are but few towns in any country of more mature years that have the tidy family residences, the commodious and well arranged public houses, the sober and industrious communities of inhabitants that the three towns in Grand Chute can boast of. There is, also, a large, flourishing division of the Sons of Temperance at Appleton. The state improvement is located on the opposite side of the river at this point, and is in the progress of construction. The country is timbered with oak, beach, hickory and maple on both sides of the river, and the soil rich and productive. It is fast filling up with good citizens from the eastern states and different portions of the west, and forms a beautiful situation for emigrants from the Old World to settle in. The price of land ranges from $2 to $10 an acre.

C.G. Atkins, Henry Blood, Charles Mory, the Phinney Brothers, and W.S. Warner were among the earliest merchants in Appleton. A New Yorker, Warner came to Wisconsin in 1844 and moved to Appleton in 1847 with his wife and two daughters. He helped chop out College Avenue, built his own house, and, with a wagon load of merchandise, set up one of the first stores in the city. Henry Blood opened his general store the same year in a small wooden building, known somewhat dubiously as Blood's Meat Market.

Hiram and James M. Phinney were brothers and business partners when they started their store in 1851. Hiram sold clothing and his brother ran an adjoining grocery store in a gabled building that would become the Henry Foster Drug Store in the early '60s. George Schmidt, another early Appleton merchant, remembered his father's stories of working at Phinney Brothers. "72 lamps and wicks had to be cleaned every morning, wood had to be chopped and hauled in for the stoves, and our customers came by oxen or team, with whole families to be outfitted for the season." In 1850 Charles Mory built the first brick store in the city, located between Morrison and Drew Streets. C.G. Adkins became a successful merchant after opening his general store in 1853.

The Green Bay *Advocate* spoke highly of the Appleton area in their January 16, 1851 edition.

"Grand Chute, Appleton and Lawesburg continue to grow and business seems in a healthy condition. We noticed many new buildings, which were constructed with a good deal of taste. The institution (Lawrence University) is in full operation and doing well. It is highly spoken of everywhere. There are many new clearings and new and neat farmhouses on the way from the Chute to Neenah. Good locations are eagerly sought after and uncleared land is sold readily for $10 to $15 per acre. This will do for a country through which, three years ago, the only road was an Indian trail."

That the editor of the Green Bay *Advocate* would report on Appleton was not unusual for there was no newspaper in the city. Libraries were almost nonexistent and there were few books to read except those brought along by Eastern settlers. Newspapers were uniquely important and well read even though they were often started as political vehicles or real estate promotions.

The four Ryan brothers moved from Fort Howard to Appleton in 1852 to set up a printing and newspaper business. John, James, Sam, Jr., and Henry Ryan hauled load after load of supplies over the treacherous Duck Creek trail from Green Bay. Their father, Colonel Samuel Ryan, helped to provide the capital for the boys to form a partnership. He also helped the night of February 10, 1853, when Samuel Ryan, Jr. used a George Washington hand press to crank out the first issue of the *Appleton Crescent,* a name derived from the bend in the Fox River. Sam served as editor, John set the type, James did composing and Henry ran errands. Up to this time the only available paper was the Green Bay *Advocate,* delivered to its subscribers by boat.

The *Appleton Crescent,* a Democratic weekly, was soon opposed by the Republican paper, *Apppleton Motor.* Later, the Motor was sold and became the *Appleton Post. The Daily Post* came off the press in 1883 and would be acquired in 1920 by J.K. Kline, A.B. Turnbill, V.I. Minahan, and H.G. Dauis. The *Crescent* was published as a daily from 1890 until January 31, 1920 when it was purchased by the Post Publishing Company and later merged with the Post to become the *Appleton Post-Crescent.*

By 1854 Appleton's trade had ballooned enormously. The $60,000 worth of goods sold in the city in 1853 soared to $150,000 by the next year.G.W. Woodward began building a whole block of brick stores on the north side of College Avenue and newcomers were settling in the outlying districts of Appleton and were raising wheat, pork and grain to be marketed in the growing city.

Seven dry goods stores were doing a brisk business in 1854, as were an independent grocery and one hardware store, one drug and grocery store, a grocery and provision store, one drug and book store, two tin shops, two paint shops, three tailor shops, one millinery shop, three cabinet ware rooms, three blacksmiths, one harness shop, a gunsmith, one market ' house, a wagon shop, one cooper and several small carpenter shops. The stirrings

of a downtown retail association began in Appleton in 1859 when most of the downtown merchants agreed to close their stores at 8 p.m. The unified closing agreement was signed by a dozen stores but did not include any of the saloons or "grog-shops", soon be governed by a city ordinance requiring:

If any person licensed to sell liquors shall open such place within the city between the hours of 11 p.m. and 5 a.m. of the day following he shall be punished by a fine of not less than $5 and not more than $25 and the costs of the suit.

The Congregationalists built a large church in 1854 and so did the Methodists. Other churches throughout the area were adding Sunday schools, and the "sabbath" was so respected that, according to historian, Thomas Ryan, Appleton was called "The Puritan Village." So rapid was the growth of the city that three saw mills worked day and night during the summer of 1854 to provide lumber to build homes and stores. Area farmers cut logs from their own land or from neighboring pine forests, but transporting lumber by way of the river was often difficult as reported by the *Crescent* on August 19, 1854:

Ladd and Letcher and Tibbits and Johnson after several weeks of hard work succeeded in getting their rafts of lumber safely moored at Grand Chute. While on Lake Winnebago they were towed by the Swan and were broken up and the logs scattered and piled upon the beach. They had great difficulty at Neenah in getting through the incomplete lock. They were also detained at Butte des Mortes. This is a roundabout way of bringing logs from the Wolf River, but it is the only way they can be brought by water until a canal is dug from the Wolf to the Fox, terminating at Appleton.

Looking east from Appleton Street along College Avenue during the 1880s, one encountered Pettibone's dry goods store (the site of Prange's today), gas street lamps, and the Dinky, the nation's first commercially successful electric trolley.

The Pettibone Peabody Company, well known in Appleton for many years, started in the early '60s as a general store and was one of the first chain store systems in the country. Chauncey J. Pettibone and George F. Peabody both possessed a talent for merchandising and were considered "men of force, character, and charming personality."

Mrs. Alden Johnston, an early Appleton resident, remembered Pettibones as "the hub of Appleton's social life", and though it was officially known as Pettibone-Peabody Company, school girls called it "Petts". "When you walked through the door of Pettibones, the first person to greet you was Ella Malone, a genial maiden lady of plumpish figure and a rich Irish wit. No one escaped her friendly greeting. Mr. Peabody usually was just around the corner for he spent much

of his time walking about, greeting customers and no doubt keeping an eye on the clerks. He was a handsome man with a neatly trimmed beard and a fine carriage. If you turned left after the greeting, you encountered "The James girls". Mamie was a genius with her fingers and there was no fad that Mamie could not create in ribbon. Her sister Eliza sold gloves. Eliza was a Gibson girl, pompadour, shirtwaist and all. Down the aisle, Mathilda or "Tillie" Whitman presided over the jewelry counter. On the second floor, Emma Martinson sold clothes that she went to New York to buy, and Millie Birch presided over the millinery. On the fence posts in the country was painted this slogan, "You'd go one hundred miles to trade at Pettibones." And if you did, you were not disappointed.

The Willy-Green Furniture Store was

one of Appleton's first in 1869. A. Schroeder and Frank Schreiter started similar establishments in 1879, and the J.R. Grassberger Company, which became Wichman's Furniture Store, was organized in 1898. Frank Schreiter's became Brettschneider's when Joseph Brettschneider, Sr. joined the firm. The store would change from Joseph Brettschneider and Sons, to Brettschneiders Sons, and finally, Brettschneider Furniture Company.

That the population increased and trade flourished in the 1860s and '70s was evident by the number of grocery stores that could be counted throughout the city and especially on College Avenue. Meat dealers, Green and Morgan, and Joseph Miller opened in 1869, John Berg and Company in 1871, Charles Leimer in 1873, followed by L. Merkel, Fred Miller, Voeck's

Market, and Hopfenspergers.

John Hopfensperger had been laying the foundation for his meat business even before the city was organized. In those days it was common for a qualified butcher to travel from farm house to farm house doing the killing and cutting for each family. John's son Andrew brought the first touch of modern retailing with the selling and delivery of meat from an ox-drawn wagon. The ox was replaced by a horse for faster service, and eventually the wagon was retired when Hopfenspergers opened their meat market on West College Avenue in the early 1900s. Starting with a small store and one delivery boy, Hopfensperger's Meat Business employed more than 70 people in their four meat markets and large sausage manufacturing plant by 1932.

There were women entrpreneurs in the

Inside the Voecks Brothers' market, Herman T. and Emil C. Voecks and their assistants stood by ready to offer their customers the finest cuts of meat available.

A steamboat visits the Marston yards on the government canal in the Appleton flats. This view looks northeast from East South River Street near the intersection with the lower Oneida. The Marston family brought tons of limestone to Appleton from their quarry south of High Cliff.

early days of business in the Fox Cities. Mrs. W.S. Cleggett opened the first beauty shop in Appleton in 1874 and took pride in her commercial fancy work as well as hair dressing. Miss M. Himebaugh started a millinery shop, as did Mrs. F.A. Adsit, Mrs. F.A. Ryan and Mrs. C.W. Billing. Well known and dependable dressmaking was done by Mrs. O.E. Freeman, Mrs. A. Ruhlander and Mrs. Robert Richards.

Kune F. Keller, father of Gustave Keller, Sr., opened a jewelry store in 1873 and from 1892 to 1922 the firm was known as K.F. Keller and Son. Two of the earliest book stores were the Post and the H.H. Himebaugh book and stationery shops. These were followed by the Fisher and Koffend Store on College Avenue in 1869, the H.F. Huelster Store in 1879, and the C.W. Greenfield Company, later sold to Ben Butler, and in 1889 to P.M. Conkey,

1852 and enlisted in 1861 in Company E, Sixth Wisconsin Infantry. He served as a lieutenant in such battles as the Second Bull Run, South Mountain, Antietam, Chancellorsville and Gettysburg. He was wounded at both South Mountain and Gettysburg and it was at the last battle that more than half of his men were killed or wounded. That he was remembered as an impressive soldier of the time was made evident by a letter he received from R.R. Dawes, Commander of the Sixth Wisconsin Regiment, and quoted by historian, Thomas Ryan:

"I can at this time see your tall form and firm step as you pressed Company E forward on a charge through that fearful storm of death. How they failed to kill you has always been a mystery to me."

an early owner of the present Conkey Book Store.

Marston Brothers Company was a mason material and fuel supply company that was founded in 1878 by Charles and Quincy Marston, and financed by their father, Captain Joseph Marston, Civil War commander of the famous Iron Brigade. The elder Marston came to Appleton in

The Marston Brothers Company survives to the present day, though it is now named the Westerfield Oil Company.

Matt Schmidt worked for Hiram Phinney for 18 years and for Joseph Spitz for 12 years before opening his own clothing store in 1898. Matt and his son, George, sold Eagle shirts, Vassar underwear, Trimble and Sunfast Hats, Interwoven

Left
Early mills at the upper dam in Appleton produced (from left to right) flour, pulp, and wood tools.

Below left
The Elm Tree Bakery on East College Avenue was an Appleton institution, operated by the Pfefferle family from 1894 to 1956 when it moved to West College Avenue. It was later purchased by Rich Products in 1970.

Hose, and Dutchess Trousers.

Heckert Shoe Company and Bohl and Maeser, familiar names in today's downtown Appleton, were early pioneers in the shoe store business. The Heckert Shoe Company was established as Heckert and Tschude, bought by Herman Heckert, Sr. in 1890, and incorporated in 1915. In 1913, progressive merchants C.F. Bohl and W. Maeser organized their footwear business. Four years later Bohl bought out his partner, and the store on North

Fire! Fire!

Fire! The word struck terror in the hearts of early settlers in the valley when water was scarce, buildings were mostly wood, and fire-fighting consisted of nothing more than bucket brigades.

In 1854 Appleton was divided into two fire districts, each with its own warden. In that same year an entire downtown business block was destroyed by fire. In 1859, a small blaze that started in a saw mill turned into an enormous conflagration burning several industrial plants to the ground. Hundreds of volunteers battled the fire for hours, but as the *Crescent* reported, "It was impossible to check the roaring flames", and within a matter of hours a paper mill, three saw mills, a rake factory, two turning mills, a bedstead factory and several other businesses were reduced to ashes. A later *Crescent* editorial deplored the fact that too many property owners "were content to insure and then take their chances on destruction by fire."

Mayor Amos Story, in his second-term inaugural address, called attention to the importance of building suitable reservoirs and pointed out that one major fire "would burn up much more than such a reservoir would cost."

Appleton's second mayor, Alvin Foster, criticized the lack of interest by city businessmen in providing funds to safeguard the community. "We need water and equipment and it is not surprising that our fire department is unequal to the task of quelling any considerable fire."

Newspapers were filled with accounts of fires that wiped out homes, hotels, businesses and factories. Fire was becoming such a menace by 1862 that outraged citizens held community meetings and demanded better protection. The volunteer Lawrence Engine Company was organized in 1863 and the city purchased a hand-operated, horse-drawn fire engine.

It proved less than adequate when within the year Appleton lost a woolen mill, an iron foundry, and seven waterfront industries to fire. In 1868 a fire tower was built, a fire bell added, and a $5 reward was offered to the first volunteer to get a team of horses to the engine house.

Thirteen business places were destroyed between Oneida and Appleton streets in 1871 in what the *Appleton Post* described as "the most extensive conflagration that has ever occurred in Appleton." The fire was finally checked by demolishing buildings in the path of the blaze. The next year, an oil explosion, caused when a young boy lit a lamp in the Manufacturers Bank building, destroyed the three-story Levake Hotel and a dozen other businesses.

The old hand engine was abandoned and a $10,000 bond issue was authorized to purchase a new fire steamer, two hose carts, 7,000 feet of hose, and to build an engine house. A second hand pumper was bought for the newly formed Grand Chute Engine Company Number Two, and by 1875 they had their own horse-drawn steamer. The companies became bitter rivals, and instead of providing improved fire protection, bickered, argued over needed equipment, and refused to help one another with fires. The building, burning, and rebuilding continued.

Bertschy's block went up in flames in 1878, and in 1881, 200 people lost their jobs and one man died in the fire that gutted the Hutchinson and Company Woolen Mill and the Appleton Chair and Bedstead Factory. So dreaded was the signal of the fire bell that the mills began sounding a warning with their whistles. One by one, they took up the call until fire fighters arrived.

A limited water supply added to the growing city's problems and by 1883 an attempt at pumping water through the city's water system was made. There was not enough water or water pressure.

Drought conditions plagued the valley in 1886 and it became known as "the year of fires." The *Post* reported that "the pillar of fire was plainly visible at Hortonville and an estimated 6,000 people gathered on the river bluffs to watch" when the Briggs, Whorton and Beveridge Sash, Door and Blind Factory burned. When fire broke out in a rag room, the Richmond Brothers Paper Mill went up in smoke at a loss of $70,000. Fire destroyed the Syme and Jones Stave Factory and the Pfeifer Tannery. Fire and job losses were so high that year that the *Post* said, "Another year of such disasters will certainly affect the prosperity of the city."

John W. Ryan, a retired fire captain from Milwaukee, helped reorganize Appleton's fire department in 1894, putting it on a full-time paid basis. Company Number One now had a hose, hook, and ladder unit. Company Two was headquartered at State and Eighth streets, and in 1898 a third company was organized and housed next to the car barns on South Oneida Street.

Captain Ryan was replaced by E.L. Anderson as chief in 1897. When Anderson was killed fighting a fire four years later, George P. McGillan became chief and remained until his retirement in 1942. Not until Chief McGillan's horse died in 1913 was the horse drawn apparatus changed to motorized units. A fire alarm system was soon installed and the department was reorganized to the two-platoon system of 24 hours on and 24 hours off duty, that survives to this day. Other valley communities fared no better. In May of 1877, Menasha lost six mill buildings and a lumber yard before a major fire could be brought under control. During dry weather many factories simply closed their doors until rain reduced the high risk of fire.

Opposite page
Although Appleton had lost another landmark, the Volksfreud Building, this 1981 fire was quickly controlled by local firefighters, unlike fires of a century ago that claimed entire city blocks and mill districts. Post Crescent *photo, OCHS*

Right
The Champion Horse Nail Company was one of the industries that bloomed on Grand Chute Island in the Appleton flats during the 1870s. The firm was capitalized at $50,000 by Dorr and Steele in 1878.

Appleton Street even today carries the name of Bohl and Maeser.

INDUSTRIES

Amos Lawrence's belief in the limitless opportunities in the Fox River Valley of Wisconsin would be a magnet drawing adventurous eastern entrepreneurs west to make the beginnings of industrial Appleton. In 1848, Lawrence built the saw mill that was to be the first industry of Appleton and would later found Lawrence College. Amos Lawrence had faith in the future of industry in Appleton when College Avenue was no more than a narrow thread of a main street littered with burned out stumps and bordered by a few wooden frame stores and houses.

As the eastern businessmen moved west local industry grew: H.S. Eggleston and G.M. Robinson's Bedstead and Cabinet Factory, The Turner Saw Mill, Gline's Wagon Shop, Lyon and Turner Livery Stables, Ketchum's Machine and Blacksmith Shop, John Turner's Appleton Brewery, the Darling Saw Mill, Dunn and Brewster Stave Factory, Turner's Chair Factory, Lawrence's Flour Mill, The Kamps Tannery, Enos Tannery, Gerard's Hub and Spoke Factory, and Clarke and Simpson's Rake Factory.

The oldest industries in Appleton relied on the surrounding forests. The Fox River Valley gained national fame with its quality woodenware including furniture, toys, wooden patterns, mill work, meat blocks, barrels, cheese, boxes, crates, and lumber. Walter W. Willson, inventor of the wood butcher block, founded Appleton Wood Products, one of the oldest industries in the city. Appleton Toy and Furniture Company was built by Michael Bauer and Daniel Walters in 1882 on land that had originally been a Menominee grant. Both Turner's chair factory and the Appleton Chair Company flourished by providing furniture for the growing market in Chicago.

Another industry naturally suited to the area was lumber. The growing communities of the Fox provided a market for millions

of board feet of white pine. The Ramsay and Jones Lumber Company (owners of large tracts of white pine timber near Menominee) started their lumber business in Appleton in 1878. Other companies soon followed, The Treat Lumber Company in 1880, and the Rose and Heath Lumber Mill, later known for both hard and soft lumber, broom handles and wagons.

The old Fourth Ward Planing Mills and the Webster Planing Company of the early 1880s became Appleton Manufacturing and Lumber Company. The Standard Manufacturing Company began in 1901 when the local lumber business was starting to decline; nevertheless, they prospered and built an addition in 1908, a lumber yard in 1918 and a saw mill in 1921. Other lumbermen were attracted by Standard Manufacturing's success. A.A. Fraser, a contractor and builder, started the Fraser Lumber Company in 1907 and S.A. Konz moved the Konz Box and Lumber Company from Black Creek to Appleton in 1920, the same year the Knoke Lumber Company was started.

Late in 1866, five businessmen launched

Above
Agricultural implements were made by a variety of Appleton firms in the 1880s and 1890s, including the Appleton Machine Company, the Eagle Manufacturing Company, and the Appleton Manufacturing Company. The Appleton Manufacturing Company advertised this Badger seeder/cultivator in 1879.

Opposite page, bottom
The first temperance society in Wisconsin was organized by the Reverend Cutting Marsh, M.D., at the south Kaukauna Stockbridge Indian mission in 1830. The temperance issue was kept alive by Yankee settlers throughout the later 1800s. Nevertheless German immigrants felt that beer was a family table beverage and established numerous breweries in the Fox Valley. The handsome George Walter Brewery, pictured, stood on the southeast corner of Walnut and Lawrence streets in Appleton from the 1890s until it was razed in 1974.

an enterprise that would have a startling impact on Appleton's future. D.R. Cameron, Joseph Noonan, Samuel and James Ryan, and R.V. Shirley pioneered one of the first paper industries when they founded the old Appleton Paper Company. With a rich supply of easily accessible rough grade timber, more pulp and paper mills moved into the Fox Cities toward the end of the 19th century. Bradner, Smith and Company of Chicago,

who operated pulp mills throughout the country, built one of their largest plants in Appleton in 1871 and called it Western Wood Pulp Mill. Their crew of 40 men worked strictly with poplar wood and helped establish pulp manufacturing in the city.

The Appleton Paper and Pulp Company was founded in 1873 and by 1880 had two Fourdrinier paper machines, one of which they claimed to be the "finest in the west."

Their daily output of white paper was six and one-half tons. A competitor, Valley Pulp and Paper Company, used what they believed to be "the finest powers on the Fox River" and built their plant on the south end of the old upper river bridge in 1879.

The valley's paper industry had planted its roots deep along the Fox River with its plentiful supply of fresh water so necessary for good papermaking. But it was in 1872 when Colonel Frambach brought the Keller groundwood process to the valley that the future of the industry was shaped. Appleton, Neenah-Menasha and Kaukauna were already producing paper from rags, but with the Keller process the focus shifted to making paper from trees.

Colonel Frambach and John Stovekin founded the Eagle Mill in Kaukauna in 1873, and according to many historians, it was the first mill with a pulp machine for grinding pulp logs. Atlas Paper and Western Wood Pulp in Appleton joined their ranks and began producing print paper from poplar logs.

The late 1800s saw several turning points in the development of the valley's

The railroads rarely made concessions to streetcar traffic. However, here the railroad trestle just north of Appleton's Prospect Avenue has an off-center support column to keep it out of the way of the earlier streetcar line on Mason Street. In most cases railroads guarded their right-of-way and would not permit a streetcar line to cross a railroad track. Courtesy, Wisconsin Electric Power Company

papermaking industry. The Civil War created a demand for news from the south and thus for newspapers. Then came a period of industrial expansion across the country and a subsequent need for paper. The first typewriter, patented in Milwaukee in 1873, and the invention of presses using continuous rolls of paper, were the seeds that sparked a tremendous growth of newspapers, publishing, advertising and a mass hunger for paper.

Appleton's paper manufacturing industry had a colorful champion in then Commander, and later, Rear Admiral

Milwaukee opposed his plan for a bridge over the company's tracks on the east side of the canal, he minced no words in informing them that he would build a bridge no matter what.

The following day railroad officials posted armed guards to patrol the railroad's right-of-way. Furious, and pacing his office in frustration, Evans decided to try a bit of diplomatic friendship. Carrying his best private stock of liquor, he met the guards on their own ground, admitted defeat, and offered to share his bottles in a gesture of peace.

Robley D. Evans. Sent to Appleton in 1891 to build the Mitscherlich sulphite mill for the Manufacturing and Investment Company (the plant later became the Interlake Division of the Consolidated Water Power and Paper Company), he set up temporary residence at the Waverly House Hotel. It was reported that President Grover Cleveland had a healthy chunk of stock in the concern and had personally commissioned Evans to build the mill.

Known as "Fighting Bob", Evans encountered many construction delays and difficulties, and fired off hotly worded telegrams to investors. He was determined to see his project through to completion. When the Lakeshore Railroad Company of

The next morning, stunned guards stared in open-mouthed horror at the wooden bridge that spanned the tracks...a bridge built in the middle of the night while the guards slept off the effects of Evan's generosity.

The Manufacturing and Investment Company was said to be the first plant in the Fox River Valley to use a "modern accounting system". Hoping to find a way to determine an accurate cost of their product, develop a system for financial operations, and discover possible leaks, Cleveland followers brought Frederick W. Taylor to Appleton. Already a business authority for labor saving methods, Taylor convinced Robley Evans to build eight large stone and cement stock pits at Lock Four on the lower river. Eight steel shells, 13 feet by 40 feet long were built and towed from Cleveland, Ohio to Green Bay. It took some maneuvering to transport the 60-ton vessels to the mill site. Getting the shells out of the river and up the high bank onto the 32-foot stone piers was another matter. It would take Herman Wildhagen, an Appleton engineer and architect to build long wooden skid-ways, pulled by a team of horses, to get the shells onto the supporting cradles.

Though Appleton entrepreneurs would

The industry would face yet another major challenge in the late 1920s with the expansion of southern mills, operating with cheaper pulp wood and labor costs. It was then that most of the valley and state paper mills curtailed the manufacturing of coarse grades and began to specialize in "fine" papers such as high quality writing and printing paper, food packaging paper, paper napkins, tissues for sanitary and home use, and container, box and carton stock.

Wool raised by area farmers was another plentiful Fox Cities crop. A local market

Appleton Woolen Mills, today known simply as Appleton Mills, was one of the local mills that adapted to the growing emphasis on the paper industry. The mills began before the Civil War and offered carding services to local sheep farmers. It later began making its own cloth for clothing and blankets. In the 1880s its wool felt became a fixture in local paper mills as part of the paper-drying process. Appleton Mills is the oldest continuing industry in Appleton.

repeatedly overcome natural obstacles with foresight and inventiveness, bureaucratic obstacles would prove to be their temporary undoing. Wisconsin lost its world leadership in the early 1900s when tariffs were removed from Canadian newsprint. Wisconsin mills could not compete with the low-priced wood and power in Canada and the reciprocal trade agreement between the two countries was a devastating blow. The state's newsprint production literally disappeared in the next 15 to 20 years. Since the ability to produce printing and writing papers had already been developed, many of the mills converted to other types of paper production and rebuilt their businesses.

was created for this commodity during the Civil War when Appleton Woolen Mills was built to manufacture Union Army uniforms. This company was the first in the county to operate with an individual electric lighting plant, and the first west of Ohio to make felts and jackets for the paper industry. In 1888, a weaving plant was added, and cashmeres and flannels became Appleton Woolen specialties. Though ownership changed repeatedly over the years, the plant always retained the name of Appleton Woolen Mills.

Appleton Superior Knitting Works was another of the earliest woolen mills. Built in 1861, incorporated in 1881, it produced only yarn until 1888 when it diversified

with the production of cloth and flannel. By 1890 the company was making papermaking felts and jackets and producing woolen clothing for the lumbermen of northern Wisconsin and Michigan.

Today's J.B. Courtney and Company on East Water Street in Appleton evolved from a combination of these early pioneers, The Courtney Wool Carding Company, the Kelly Knitting Company, and the Spearing Knitting Works. The Zwicker Knitting Mills, founded in 1907 by German immigrant Robert Emil Zwicker, is still doing business in present day Appleton under the leadership of Thomas Zwicker, great grandson of the founder.

Many types of small industry were to try their luck in the valley during this period. O.P. Conklin started a boot and shoe factory in 1879 after leasing their site and power from a firm that had failed to make

a go of steel horseshoe nails. Appleton Wire Works was founded in 1885 by Scotsman William Buchanan and his factory on North Lawe Street turned out 2000 feet of woven wire each week in the first year of operation. This feat was accomplished on four hand-operated looms specially designed by Buchanan and operated by Scottish workmen highly skilled in the craft of wire weaving.

J.J. Plank had his own ideas about the use of wire. After training at the Appleton Screen Plate Company, Plank decided to start his own company. In 1908, he rented two rooms, hired a young girl to fabricate tiny copper wire letters and a man to make wire trusses for rolls, and called it the J.J. Plank Company—one of the few wire industries to make dandy rolls.

Even flax had its day when valley soil was found to be excellent for that crop. In 1880 the Fleming and Company Flax Mills

Left
One of the transitional local crops was flax, as pioneer Fox Valley farmers began the switch from wheat to dairying. Fleming's Linen Mills were still going strong on Appleton's Grand Chute Island in 1892. Lawrence University's Main Hall can be seen behind the mills.

Opposite page
When Lawrence University's debate team won an interstate competition in Denver in 1900, most of the student body crammed into two Appleton streetcars to welcome the team home. Courtesy, Wisconsin Electric Power Company

opened at their location on the lower end of the water power canal. It would take the company only a year to begin the manufacture of agricultural implements with the production of 200 horse-hoe cultivators. The next year would see the production of automatic seeders.

TEMPERANCE AND CULTURE
Many of the easterners, like Joseph Stowe, Daniel Huntley, and R.R. Bateman, that settled in Appleton and the Fox Valley had a puritanical New England background. They were industrious, hard working, enterprising individuals determined to forge a community that would fit their values and ideals. Because the imbibing of liquor had no place in their lifestyle and because it was "the city's responsibility to preserve the character and morals of the students of Lawrence College," temperance groups and anti-liquor laws were the issue of the day.

There was hardly a mayor that took office without addressing the temperance issue. In 1854 the common council passed an ordinance prohibiting the

"introduction, storing, depositing, keeping in store, in deposit or on hand, or having in possession within the corporate limits of Appleton, any spirituous, vinous, malt, fermented, mixed or intoxicating liquors or exchanging the same, or for any species of traffic."

The Civil War affected the two temperance organizations, the Good Templars, organized in 1858, and the Sons of Temperance, chartered in 1851. Alcohol had been used by many to ease physical, as well as psychological pain during the dreadful war. The liquor ordinance, so strongly supported in 1854, was a dead issue 11 years later when the council voted its repeal. Another factor influencing the change came with immigrants whose cultural background included the partaking of beer, wine, and sometimes, hard liquor with meals or for special celebrations.

In 1868 the grand opening of a downtown saloon was marked by an all-out brawl which resulted in several broken bones and assorted bruises. Soon after the council posted a "black-list" on city streets naming individuals who could not handle their liquor and who were known to drink too much, too often. No one was allowed to sell or provide any alcoholic beverage to

The home of Augustus Ledyard Smith was one of the first houses on the east side of town to be electrified, using power from the east-end Vulcan Street hydroelectric plant in 1882. The Smith Home was later torn down to make way for the present Lawrence University Memorial Union building.

such persons. In addition, the Methodist church sponsored a non-drinking pledge and circulated it throughout the city.

LIGHT IN THE VALLEY

While some Appletonians were concerned about temperance others were working to bring innovative advances to the "river city". In 1865 Fox Valley citizens had been excited about the newly incorporated Appleton Gas Light Company. Capital was fixed at $200,000. Stock sold for $100 a share, with a goal of $10,000 to start operations. But when the first gas well was dug, it provided a disappointingly small supply of gas.

Producing gas by destructive distillation of coal was started in 1877 and it took just four months to break ground, put a plant in operation and lay three miles of pipes. By October of that year the city's leading businesses were using gas. Gas lamps were installed at Turner Hall and would be lit for the first time at a gala "gaslight ball" on October 26. It turned out to be a romantic, but somewhat dim evening when the lights burned faintly because of air in the pipes. When repeated a few days later

the experiment was more successful.

The Appleton Gas Light Company manufactured gas for industrial and home use, and in 1886, a gas ordinance was adopted by the city council. The company was not to charge more than 33 cents per thousand feet. The Wisconsin Natural Gas and Mining Company went into business that same year and struck gas at a depth of 50 feet. Even though the well came in at an exciting volume, its success was short-lived. And though the Appleton Gas Company signed a contract with the city in 1890 for 160 gas lamps at $20 each, by the turn of the century those gas lamps would be rendered primitive by the extraordinary invention of an extraordinary man.

As soon as the announcement came that Thomas Edison had found a way to put the mysterious power of electricity to practical use with a demonstration of his electric light at Menlow Park, New Jersey, believers dreamt of wealth and a world lighted by electricity.

Appleton financier and industrialist, H.J. Rogers, was so fascinated by the idea that he purchased the Edison patent-licensee rights for the Fox Valley without even seeing the product or its demonstration. In July, 1882, Rogers brought a Western Edison Light Company engineer to Appleton to explain the lighting system to city businessmen. Rogers' enthusiasm was so contagious that bankers Augustus L. Smith and Charles Beveridge and blast furnace owner H.D. Smith ordered two Edison Type "K" dynamos, each with the generating capacity of 250 lamps or 12-1/2 kilowatts. By mid-August contracts were signed, a plant built and equipment installed. One generator was connected to the water wheels at Rogers' pulp beater mill. Wiring was completed at Rogers' home and another of his mills and the new invention was ready to be tested. On September 27 the power was turned on and everyone held their breath in readiness. But no lights appeared. The plant failed to function. But three days later electric lights glowed in Appleton, making the financiers home and the mills "bright as day." The Rogers' house on West Prospect Street was the first home in the west to be exclusively lighted by electric lamps. Within three months of Rogers' introduction to electric lights, the first hydroelectric central station in the world began business in Appleton.

At first, the business of hydroelectricity was makeshift and unreliable. The first power plant was built in 1882 and W.D. Kurz, who worked with A.C. Langstadt, was the first electrical engineer. The central station, located on the river between the two mills of Appleton Paper and Pulp Company, was a small frame shack. The two wire 160 volt Edison dynamos were driven by water wheels, which also powered the paper mill. Because of the varying load and the change in speed, the voltage was far from constant, and sometimes so high that all the lamps in the circuit burned out. It proved to be an expensive problem as each of the 550 lamps cost $1.60. A separate water wheel for the dynamo had to be installed to get better results. Another powerhouse was built in November and the voltage improved.

The plant now had five customers; two more residences, a blast furnace, and the Waverly Hotel. They were served directly from the dynamo, and Kurz, who had become plant superintendent, did everything possible to insure good service. Regulators had not yet been developed and voltage was judged by the pilot lamps. If the operator in the powerhouse had good eyesight, there were no customer complaints about the brightness of the lights. There were no voltmeters, ammeters, instruments, fuses, or lightning protection. The copper wires had little insulation and even a slight disturbance could short out the circuit. When this happened every available man was sent out to trace wires, and service was suspended until the short was located.

The cities along the Fox River were among the most highly industrialized and urbanized in the state, and were a promising market for electric development. If the technicalities of transmitting could be improved, the area had the potential of becoming one giant electric service unit. Any company that got a foothold in Appleton could easily expand, connecting all of the Fox River Valley.

But the Appleton Edison Light Company, incorporated in May of 1883, was having more than technical difficulties. More money was going out than coming in. The citizenry of Appleton found the electric light to be beautiful, novel and inexpensive because the new company, overwhelmed by confusion, uncertainty and change, sold its product below cost. By the end of 1885, the company was over its head in debt, overdrawn at the bank, and the stockholders' $24,000 investment had not yielded one cent in dividends.

Appleton Edison began an extensive advertising campaign and improved their service with a new 190-kilowatt plant, including regulating equipment, fuses, and a three-wire distribution system. Electrolytic customer meters were added in 1888 and the next year they went to 24-hour service and outdoor arc lights. As service became

When Appleton Judge Joseph Harriman saw them in Montgomery, Alabama, he was convinced that a street car company in his home town would be a marvelous improvement and net a fortune for its backers.

Judge Harriman became president of the Appleton Electric Street Railway Company in 1885, formed with the backing of F.W. Harriman, Norman Clark, Joseph Koffend, Sr., T.W. Orbison, Captain N.M. Edwards, K.W. Cook and R.W. Lunt. A franchise was granted, a plant built and road work started in January with Van Depoele and his assistant, Elmer Morris, supervising the construction. The five open cars, specially ordered (complete with handsome wicker benches) from the Pullman Company, made their four-mile run from Riverside cemetery to the corner of State and Prospect streets on Circus Day in 1885. The circus, however, was quickly forgotten as the onlookers and circus performers ran to the street to view the history-making event.

Besides the Cemetery-Junction Line, as it was called, a track was originally laid on Appleton Street from the Chicago and

more reliable, the number of customers increased and the company began to make money.

FIRST ELECTRIC STREET RAILWAY
Meanwhile another significant development was taking place that would bring Appleton the first commercially successful electric street railway in America on January 14, 1886. While dozens of other inventors had failed, Charles J. Van Depoele began to demonstrate his electric street car invention in 1883 in Chicago. In the next two years, he took the cars to Toronto, South Bend, and Minneapolis.

Left
The 1889 streetcar line from
Appleton Street down to
lower Oneida was designed to
pick up passengers from the
railroad depots in the flats,
but the grade was too steep to
be practical. Appleton's first
large apartment building
appears on the right.
Courtesy, Wisconsin Electric
Power Company

Opposite page
Joseph Harriman served in a
variety of public offices,
including Appleton mayor
and county judge. In addition
to developing local parks and
real estate, Judge Harriman
founded the first commercially
successful electric streetcar line
in America. His home is
pictured at left in 1887.

Northwestern Depot to the Milwaukee and
St. Paul Depot across the river. When it
was discovered that the bridge was an
extremely dangerous point of crossing and
that teams of horses had to pull the cars
up the steepest part of the hill on
Appleton Street, the line between the
depots was discontinued leaving the
Cemetery-Junction Line as the only street
car route in the city.

As the use of streetcars increased, the
open cars were replaced by warmer and
more practical closed cars. But there were
still annoying complications to this mode
of travel. With rails laid over unpaved
streets, the cars often "jumped the tracks."
Though the cars had been constructed of
lightweight materials in anticipation of this
problem and could easily be righted by the
strength of two men, the process was time
consuming. Also, the street car motors were
set on a platform built on the front of the
cars and turntables had to be built at each
end of the line so that the motorman

could turn the car by hand, another
ingenious but frustrating delay. Some of
the other technical difficulties were not so
easily solved. Operations were suspended
during storms because there was no
lightning protection, and snows had to be
hand shoveled from the tracks if the cars
were to operate at all in the winter
months.

Although service was unpredictable and
slow the Appleton Electric Street Railway
Company made money. But by 1891 the
newness had worn off and investors were
faced with having to either modernize, sell,
or go bankrupt. They decided to sell and
in 1891 Smith and Beveridge put up the
money to consolidate the lighting company
and street railway companies and called it
Appleton Edison Electric Company.
Edison, the parent company, put John I.
Beggs on the board of directors of the
Appleton Company. A Vermonter who
had the reputation of a penny-pincher and
a shrewd businessman, Beggs would,

Appleton electrical pioneers Frank and Will Kurz (left) and their brother-in-law Al Langstadt (center, wearing derby) try out the new Sprague trolley, Appleton's second type of electric streetcar. Courtesy, Wisconsin Electric Power Company

eventually, control the electric utility industry throughout Wisconsin.

Confident of continuing success, the electric company began improvements for the street railway. Sensing a golden opportunity, the Appleton Gas Company cut their rates to $1 per thousand cubic feet, undermining electric rates. A few months later, A.C. Langstadt, M.H. Croswell and John Peterson organized the Citizens Electric Light and Power Company, and installed a modern polyphase alternating current light and power system. The Edison Company cut its rates from one cent to one-half cent per lamp hour but it had already lost too much to its competitors.

Edison credit fell apart and the company was forced to look for a buyer. Smith & Beveridge hoped to sell out to a competitor wanting a franchise for an electric interurban railway from Oshkosh, through Appleton, to Green Bay. Neenah and Menasha held back in selling their

franchises, sure that the interurban line would reroute trade to larger cities. The delay in negotiations was too much for Edison and in January, 1896, Appleton Edison Electric Company went bankrupt.

Determined to persevere, Augustus Smith bought back the property and established the Appleton Electric Light and Power Company. The next year he bought out the competing Citizens Company. Tragically, just as he was succeeding, Smith's plans, literally, went up in smoke as fire totally destroyed the generating plant.

It took a group of Milwaukee capitalists led by F.G. Bigelow, B.K. Miller, H.C. Payne, and Charles Pfister to bring the interurban railway plan to fruition. The group bought the Neenah and Menasha Electric Railway Company in 1897, called it the Fox River Valley Electric Railway Company, and extended its lines to Appleton and Kaukauna. When another fire destroyed the power plant in 1900, the

Appleton company provided emergency connection and power. The emergency underscored the feasibility of a merger between the two companies, and John Beggs and the Milwaukee investors formed the Wisconsin Traction, Light, Heat, and Power Company. The following year that company bought out both the Appleton Electric Light and Power and the Fox River Valley Electric Railway Company. A last-ditch merger of the Appleton Gas Company and the Neenah-Menasha Gas and Electric proved futile and within three years they too sold to the Wisconsin company. By 1904 John Beggs controlled the supply of electric, traction and gas service in and between Appleton, Neenah and Menasha.

WISCONSIN'S FIRST PHONE
An Appleton banker, Alfred Galpin, Jr. again, demonstrated astute judgment in regard to a new American invention. After hearing of Alexander Graham Bell's success, Galpin wrote to the inventor and received this reply from Bell's father-in-law:

Washington, D.C., February 29, 1877, Mr. A. Galpin, Jr., Appleton, Wisconsin.

Dear Sir:

Your note making inquiries in regard to the telephone has been received. Negotiations are now in progress for the introduction of the telephone to the public. As soon as these are completed I will give you the particulars you desire. Yours truly, Gardiner G. Hubbard.

Appleton is credited with having the first telephone in service in Wisconsin, and establishing one of the first telephone exchanges in the United States.
The December, 1926 "Wisconsin Magazine of History" featured an article titled, "The History and Development of the Telephone in Wisconsin" by Harry Barsantee, in which he wrote,

In 1890 Appleton turned to Sprague cars. The Combined Light and Traction Company's new streetcars are shown on the Pacific Street Bridge. Courtesy, Wisconsin Electric Power Company

"The history of the telephone in Wisconsin dates back to 1877, although exact dates are conflicting and few....It seems hardly conceivable that the telephone should have been put to practical use in Wisconsin in the very year following its invention and practically as soon as it was accepted in the East; yet in the year 1877 a banker in Appleton by the name of Alfred Galpin made the plunge by connecting his bank and residence. His was reputed to be the first telephone ever used in Wisconsin."

Alfred Galpin III in his "Portrait of a Father" in the same magazine's summer issue of 1980, said,

"Very early in 1877 father constructed with his own hands a pair of telephones and wired them to connect our home with his office in the bank, contiguous to a drugstore on College Avenue. The drugstore promptly followed up this initiative by establishing a service connecting their store with one then with two more Appleton physicians. From this grew the establishment in 1880 of the Appleton Telephone Company. Appleton honored father's exploit during the second centennial celebration in 1976 by posing a commemorative plaque."

Employees of the
APPLETON EDISON LIGHT CO.
July 1891

The first telephone line was strung from Benoit and Bleser Drug Store on East College Avenue to Dr. J.T. Reeve's office and to the homes of Louis Benoit and Dr. A.H. Levings. The first telephone exchange opened with Miss Kate Hollihan as the first operator. She was promoted to manager when Benoit died in 1881 and two years later the exchange was large enough to move out of the drug store to the floor above.

The telephone was both a novelty and a lifesaver for Appleton residents. When one of the first phones was rigged up at George Spaulding's house, people came from all over to get a look at "the new fangled thing you talk into." Dr. J.T. Reeve liked to tell the story of how he and E.P. Humphrey, editor of the *Appleton Post* used to dial up their phones, stand in front of facing windows and talk to each other from across the street.

Those who had telephones were willing to share, but stage fright seemed to be a common ailment for first-time-users. When the second party was "rung up," communication established, and the receiver handed to the caller, he would become confused, flustered, and not able to utter a word.

The importance of the telephone was evident the day Judge Joseph Harriman was working in his yard and stepped on the handle of a scythe. The blade flew up, causing a deep cut in his side and severing an artery. He was able to get to the house, call Dr. Leving's office, and as the story was told and retold, the doctor arrived just in time to save the judge's life.

Telephones, electric lights, and street cars were remarkable yet obvious changes in the every day life of the Fox Cities at the turn of the century. But there was also a profound change that could not be observed day to day. The pace of life was speeding up and the progress of science and invention was just one of the connections, just one more strong bond that reflected the optimism and pulsing life of the valley's people as cities became industrialized, machinery came to farms,

and Fox Citians considered themselves literate and thinking in their quest for profit, and economic and social betterment. It was a time of almost constant transition as the emphasis changed from colonizing to accomplishment, as the valley adjusted from settling in to setting up for the growth and success that was sure to come.

And come they did. Mayor R.R. Bateman was chosen president of the Friends of Freedom. Democrat Chauncey Kellogg gave an exciting speech and set aside his partisan feelings to "uphold national honor." James Phinney became so emotional he could barely speak. T.R. Hudd "delivered an eloquent and powerful talk", and George H. Marston received a standing ovation for his patriotic words. The Star Spangled Banner was sung and the following resolution read:

"We the Union-loving people of the city of Appleton, hereby pledge our lives, our fortunes and our sacred honor in defense of the rights and liberties of the United States of America; we deem it our privilege as well as our bounded duty to uphold the pure principles of our republican government; to maintain the rights of each citizen in person and property; to uphold our banner, the Stars and Stripes, against all opposition, come from what quarter it may."

Above
Wisconsin's first telephone was built in Appleton in 1877, and by 1917 local operators were "at home" with their work. Switchboards, especially in rural areas, were often monitored by women at their homes.

Opposite page
Employees of the Appleton Edison Light Company in July of 1891 were (from left) Albert Langstadt, William Carpenter, Paul Radtke, August Meyer, Harry Knox, Kenneth Knox, and John Peterson. Courtesy, Wisconsin Electric Power Company

Strong Bonds

The 1860s brought the promise of great prosperity and growth to the river cities. Industries were flourishing. Retail business was expanding. In Appleton, the Democratic newspaper, the Crescent called Abraham Lincoln "a handsome sucker gentleman" and urged residents to vote for Stephen Douglas. Although Douglas outpolled Lincoln in Outgamie County, Appleton gave Lincoln a majority of 54 votes.

The threat of war hung heavy. People talked of little else as they went about their daily business.

Previous page
The Appleton Juvenile Band
kept people entertained in
1898.

Initially, slavery was not the issue so much as secession. A feature article quoting Senator Stephen Douglas of Illinois in the May 25, 1861 Appleton *Crescent* best expresses the prevailing attitude:

"The present secession movement is the result of a conspiracy more than a year ago. They used the slavery question as a means to accomplish the end. They decided to break up the Union, and used the election of Mr. Lincoln as a mere excuse...the conspiracy to break up the Union is known to all. There can be but two sides. Every man must be on the side of the Union states or against it...there can be no neutral ground...nor will the North be divided...the conspirators have expected to have a divided North and a united South. War does exist. The government must be maintained. Its enemies must be overthrown."

When confederate gunboats opened fire on Fort Sumter in April of 1861, the impact was felt all the way to the valley of the Fox. With President Lincoln's immediate call for 75,000 volunteers, Fox Cities Democrats and Republicans alike "rallied for the Union" and a call, signed by 150 citizens of Appleton was circulated. It said:

"THE UNION FOREVER! RALLY FOR THE UNION! Citizens of the Republic; lovers of your country; all who love liberty and hate tyranny; all who have in your veins a drop of the old revolutionary blood or who have adopted United States as their home, come together tonight at Adkins Hall. Treason has already shown itself at our very capital; has seized upon the nation's defenses and taken possession of her arms and munitions of war; has insulted and trampled upon her flag, the Star Spangled Banner; and contemplates the destruction of the

Union; come then and with word and deed assist in restricting his anarchy. God will protect the right."

Patriotism was contagious and the war was but two months old when the following letter arrived;

To the Friends of Freedom in Appleton...We the undersigned chiefs of the Oneidas in view of the fact that some of our ancestors aided in the achievement of the liberty of this country, costing them their lives and a desire to perpetuate the celebration of the Fourth of July in a patriotic way, we make an appeal to you, to donate us a flag to be raised on that day. We make this appeal; first, because we do not feel able to purchase the material to make one; and second, because there are none of our people that know how to make one if we had the material. In conclusion we would say that in case of necessity we are ready to stand by your side and die, too, if need be, that the "star spangled banner may wave o'er the land of the free and the home of the brave." John Cornelius, Elyh Scanado, Jacob Cornelius, Baptist Scanadoah, Adam Swamp; Chiefs of the Oneidas, Oneida, June 24, 1861."

City bands and a wildly cheering, patriotic crowd escorted the new recruits and their compatriots out of Appleton in a noisy procession from College Avenue to the Chicago and Northwestern railroad station on Appleton Street. The first Appleton man to enlist in the Union Army was Louis Schintz, 21. Born in Zurich, Switzerland, he came to America as a 12 year old boy and eventually moved to Oshkosh to work as a clerk for his brother Theodore, who was a magistrate and notary public. In January, 1861 he came to Appleton to work for Perry H. Smith but within four months enlisted in Company E, Second Wisconsin Infantry.

Companies were organized throughout the valley and by June, fifty Outagamie County men had enlisted in Chicago and Fond du Lac. Since the Federal government was short of supplies, each valley community outfitted its own soldiers. Ceremonies were repeated again and again as city after city sent its men to war. Comfort-bags and other necessities were handed out by "ladies assembled in a line, each armed with a big bouquet and encouraging words for the noble cause in which recruits were about to be engaged."

Women in the valley were used to working for missionary and sewing societies for their respective churches and when war came they met in large groups to provide clothing, quilts, lint, bandages and comfort-bags for valley soldiers. Making lint required stretching a piece of linen or old table cloth over a plate and scraping it with a sharp knife into a fluffy pile of lint to be used as absorbent cotton in field hospitals. The comfort-bag or "hussy" was a small fabric case containing needles, white sewing cotton, black linen thread, buttons, yarn and pins. If the society could afford it they also added a small bottle of quinine for medicinal purposes.

Fox Valley women knit mittens, gloves and socks throughout the war and also collected vegetables to be sent to the army as "anti-scorbutics" to prevent scurvy. Begging committees were organized to canvas the area, and aid societies packed vegetables and pickles and sauerkraut to be shipped to the war weary troops.

Samuel Ryan, Jr., editor of the *Crescent* used his newspaper to ask for volunteers for his "Appleton Invincibles." He was quick to announce that soldiers' pay had been increased by Congress, that Wisconsin would give $5 to their families, and Appleton would support families of volunteers during their absence.

Louis Schintz was luckier than many of the Appleton recruits who followed his lead in enlisting for the Union cause. Schintz fought in several Southern battles before being wounded at the Battle of Bull Run. His survival is attributed to the well placed suspender buckle that fortuitously deflected a potentially fatal Confederate bullet. Schintz was discharged in February 1863 to return to Appleton and his job with Perry Smith. Rev. H.A. Miner of Menasha recalled the anxious days of war:

I remember the meetings for enlisting recruits, the patriotic speeches and the shouts that went up as one after another enrolled his name to go to the front. Then the drilling and the parting scenes as company after company left for the scene of conflict; then the awful waiting for news. The daily mail reached us from the South at night just after supper. A crowd would gather at the postoffice and one man would stand on a box and read the latest from the front. What anxiety to learn the fate of our Menasha boys. Our church was largely represented. I think the names of over twenty were printed in large letters and taced upon the front of the gallery, so each Sabbath they were remembered and prayers offered for their fidelity and safe return to home and friends. When news came of the death of anyone his name was wreathed in mourning.

Valley citizens had been confident that the war would not last long, but by 1863 this shining patriotism had dulled. Draft insurance associations were launched to insure draftees against having to go to war by providing substitutes for a fee of $25. Union Leagues were organized to combat the war resistance, and even though their meetings were held in secret, the leagues had more than 100 members in Appleton alone.

When the glorious news arrived that Richmond had been captured from the rebels in late March, the *Crescent* reported:

"Never since our residence here have we seen such a crazy, joyful company. The old gun was brought out and thundered the news; the bells rang

out a joyful peal; flags floated in the breeze and excessive jollity reigned. At night everything went with looseness. Captain Marston had out his cavalry; the boys lighted the city with bonfires; the firemen paraded the streets with their machine to the music of fife and drum and the streets and sidewalks were lined with a happy crowd who made merry until a late hour."

When the war ended in 1865, with the surrender of General Robert E. Lee, the news triggered celebrations up and down the river.

But the cheers had hardly faded when important news again circulated in the valley. President Lincoln had been shot. Businesses were closed and draped in black. Cannons sounded and flags drooped at half mast. From nine in the morning to four o'clock in the afternoon, on the day of Lincoln's funeral guns were fired at half hour intervals. The continuous tolling of mournful church bells was eerily silenced at 12 noon. Valley residents wore black badges as they mourned the assassinated president and the men who never came home.

Following the war, powerful social and economic changes brought a dynamic upsurge in the growth of the Fox River Valley. Cities throbbed with the power of mills and reverberated with activity as farmers came to town with produce, businesses expanded, fortunes were made, and a solid foundation was laid for a golden age of growth in the valley.

Education was a possession highly prized by the hard working people who had chosen to settle the area. Schools were a priority in every community—no matter how large or small. Like the city itself, Appleton's public system grew from the separate areas of Grand Chute, Lawesburg, and Appleton, and would, eventually, be divided into four wards.

Lawesburg had the advantage of Lawrence College's resources and, consequently, did not have a public school until 1857 and a public school building

until 1881. Grand Chute formed their own school district in 1852 with a one-story frame school house that was soon replaced by the Hercules building. By 1877 the city of Appleton had four grades: grammar, first, second, and third. Mary Hillard became Appleton's first woman teacher, and her monthly pay, was $13.63—about half the amount received by male teachers at this time.

As early as 1870 the city had one of the first kindergartens west of the Allegheny Mountains. A private school that was well-known beyond Appleton, the Pestalozzian Institute was established through the efforts of Anson Ballard. The Institute embraced the brilliant teaching methods of Johann Heinrich Pestalozzi, a Swiss educator who contributed greatly to the development of theory and practice in education. Pestalozzi believed that education should be based on the natural

Veterans of the Grand Army of the Republic paraded in Appleton as part of a Civil War veterans' reunion in 1898 (left). In the same year a new generation of young men embarked for service in the Spanish-American War (below left).

Carrie Morgan, an outstanding educator and school administrator, served the Appleton Public School System for 38 years. When she died in 1964, she was 100 years old.

development of the child, and that the moral and physical aspects of that development were as important as the intellectual. He felt that a student learned best by using his senses and by discovering things independently. Pestalozzi's book, "How Gertrude Teaches Her Children", published in 1801, remains a classic in the field of education.

At this same time two other kindergartens were started in private homes, but it would take Carrie Morgan as superintendent of schools in 1898 to see that kindergarten became a formal part of the public school system.

Carrie Morgan's family came to Appleton from Plattesburg, New York in

the late 1860s. Carrie graduated from the second district high school in Appleton and received her Bachelor of Literature degree from the University of Wisconsin in just three years at a time when few women attended college. After her graduation, she taught language for five years at the high school in Neenah. Forced to leave the classroom at her mother's death, Carrie Morgan continued her work in the field of education from an office in her home. She was elected to the post of superintendent of Appleton schools in 1894 and served until 1925. When she resigned she became secretary and purchasing agent for the Appleton Board of Education. Her office served as Appleton high school and even later, city hall.

Carrie Morgan had given 38 years of dedicated service to the Appleton Public School System by the time of her death in 1864 at the age of 100. When she began teaching, a woman made $13.63 per month and worked in a system that, until 1943, restricted the marital status of female

strong group of advocates for vocational education helped to found the Appleton Vocational School which would later become the Fox Valley Technical Institute. Known as "the lighted schoolhouse on the hill" the institute was the first school in the United States built for vocational purposes. Neenah's first school was opened

The old Appleton Vocational School sat on the bluff east of Oneida Street (the present site of the Elks Clubhouse). The school later became the Fox Valley Technical Institute and has moved northwest of Appleton.

teachers to single or widowed. Her unselfish dedication to the development of the minds of Appleton's children is even more profound in light of the social constraints of her time.

After Wisconsin's Compulsory Education Law of 1879, Appleton built seven elementary schools, and was one of the first communities in the state to have a public high school.

Morgan so strongly believed in the need for early schooling that she personally supervised a house-to-house canvas, talking to parents with children of kindergarten age, in order to arouse public opinion and bring the issue to a vote.

In 1918, Carrie Morgan along with a

in 1847 when the community was less than a year old. It started as a grocery store and was converted into a one-room schoolhouse for 12 students and their teacher, Carolyn Boynton. Her salary was $6.00 per month. The first high school, organized in 1876 graduated Jessie Cooke, Nellie Herrick, Minnie Gittins, Della Brown, Mamie Ford, Fanny Wheeler and Jackson Fuller.

The first school in Menasha was located in lawyer Elbridge Smith's frame house on Water Street in 1848. Hattie Frost was the teacher and she was paid a shilling a week for each scholar. A public school was established a year later and hired Mrs. Henry Alden to teach. Some of the

Right and opposite page
Early classes at the vocational
school taught students subjects
such as sewing (right) and
furniture finishing (opposite
page).

students would remain in Menasha and become leading citizens.

Henry Hewitt, Jr.'s father was a stern penny-pincher and refused to buy his son an arithmetic book. Young Henry had to borrow Charles Donaldson's book and he was a determined scholar. By the time he was 13 years old he had earned $12,000 as a contractor for a lock and dam on the upper Fox River. He speculated in land, became a bank cashier and eventually left Menasha to become a successful land speculator in Wasington.

Frank J. Sensenbrenner was born and educated in Menasha, became an expert bookkeeper and moved up the ladder at Kimberly-Clark Company. From stockholder to vice president to general manager to president to chairman of the board.

Responding to the papermaking expertise of area residents, the prestigious Institute of Paper Chemistry was founded in Appleton in 1929 by Ernest Mahler, Dan K. Brown, L.M. Alexander, D.C.

Everst, U. Strange, M.A. Wertheimer, and Henry M. Wriston. The independent, privately-supported graduate school is the only one of its kind in the world and offers a master of science and a doctor of philosophy degree. It is an international research center and central information agency for science and technology in the manufacture and use of pulp paper and paperboard. Its Dard Hunter Museum displays the remarkable evolution of paper making and houses the largest collection of paper history in the world.

Just as Lawrence University played a major role in the founding of Appleton, it continues to exert its influence on the valley. The college attracts students from all over the world, enriching the area with a unique cultural mix. Since the early 1860s when the Literary and the Phoenix societies of the college opened the valley's door to the outside world of art, literature and music, the university has stimulated art and culture in the valley. James Sutherland, former mayor of Appleton describes

Connections

In 1900 Appleton boasted a population of almost 16,000 and "educational facilities unequaled in any other city of its size in the state," J.F. Fuller wrote in The First Congregational Church, a chronicle of the first 50 years of the church. Fuller went on:

"In this year of 1900 the city has 14 church organizations with buildings and four mission chapels, besides other religious organizations not yet provided with buildings. Over one million dollars have been invested here for school and church purposes. It has over 200 independent manufacturing establishments representing a great variety of commodities. Its facilities for traffic by steam and electric roads and steamboats are ample. Besides the college and four public school libraries, it also has a Free Public Library and Reading Room, well patronized. It sustains six weekly newspapers and two dailies, in addition to other regularly published periodicals. It has three national banks and mercantile interests of all kinds are represented. It is the seat of government for the county of Outagamie."

In the cities and villages up and down the river people were talking about "progress", "social betterment", and "modernity" as the Fox Cities faced the 20th century. Kaukauna policemen were now wearing full uniforms and the fire engine house had been equipped with a steam heater. You could buy a new Rand McNally map of Wisconsin at the Kaukauna Times office, and a bottle of Dr. King's New Discovery For Consumption (a cure for coughs, colds, asthma, bronchitis, croup, and all throat and lung diseases,) at Charlesworth's Drug Store. The first bottle was free. On August 1, 1902 *The Kaukauna Times* reported that Julius Kuehn had put in the first cement sidewalk in front of his business block on Second Street. The paper called it "a substantial improvement. A cement walk is by far the cheapest in the long run and is generally being adopted in all of the larger cities. When once laid in the proper form, it will remain for a lifetime. The life of a boardwalk is only seven years, at best."

Menasha had grown to over 7,000

people by 1900 and could well be labeled an industrial city with its 30 factories and 2,500 working residents, 1,600 employed in the wooden ware industry. Over 100 telephones were in use and Menashans could travel back and forth between Menasha, Appleton and Neenah on the Interurban Electric Line. The city dock was a regular stopping place for many steamboats and the railway not only provided transportation, but brought in goods and dispersed manufactured products from the valley. In the summer months, people from all over the country came to Menasha to vacation at the popular Robert's Resort.

John Roberts had purchased land on the Fox River, facing Lake Winnebago, in 1875

and built the resort, which opened on May 30, 1877. The most striking feature of the two-story hotel was a second-floor veranda for viewing both the river and the lake. The resort had 35 rooms, 3 cottages, a billiard room, a smoking room, an elegant restaurant, and a dining room for banquets. Roberts maintained a herd of cows and a flock of chickens in order to supply his own meat, milk, and eggs. The popular vacation spot also offered golf, tennis, and croquet tournaments and a fancy dress ball every Saturday night.

Menashans could order lemon, sassparilla or vanilla sodas at druggist John Rosch's soda fountain, and could read two daily newspapers; *The Daily Press* and the *Evening Breeze,* later to become the *Twin*

City News Record. In 1905 local papers proudly reported the completion of Menasha's all-diesel generating plant—the first in the world. The plant provided electric power for the community's carbon incandescent street lights and was serving private customers by 1911.

Neenah, too, was beginning to think as a city and of its responsibilities to its residents. As the 19th century came to a close each Neenah household depended on a rainwater supply collected in a basement cistern. Private wells provided water for drinking and cooking. When summer dry seasons threatened the water supply, residents used untreated lake water. Public pressure for a city water system resulted in a city well and city mains in 1893. The

Teddy (the horse) poses with members of the Rippl family in front of their successful Menasha business in 1914. Courtesy, Elisha D. Smith Public Library, Menasha

water was so hard that it clogged the pipes and discolored dishes and clothes, but Neenah residents lived with the inconvenience for 40 years. When Menasha installed a treatment plant to filter and purify river water, the Neenah

Advancement Committee was organized, and in 1932 asked voters to support a proposal for a city water system. It was defeated by a margin of two to one. In 1934 the committee established a water commission and built a small water plant.

Members of the commission delivered water to individual homes, urging residents to try it for washing and cooking. They provided drinking water for business groups and for organizational luncheon and dinner meetings. In April of 1936

every ward in the city voted in favor of the new water system and by February of 1937 Neenah had its own water treatment plant.

Small businesses flourished in Neenah at the turn of the century, as did the industries that would provide a solid economic strength for years to come. George Schmidt's cigar manufacturing plant was housed in a brick building at 112 North Commercial Street and, when sales were good, employed 40 men. Charles "Charley" Bergstrom had a blacksmith shop on North Commercial Street and also sold carriages in the 1880s and 1890s, but with the demise of the horse and buggy, Charley was forced to sell bicycles and, finally, cars.

In 1901 the Banta Publishing Company was incorporated, and in 1919 it's division, the George Banta Paper Company, was renamed the Central Paper Company. W.L. Davis sold his Winnebago Paper Mills to D.W. Bergstrom and his son, John, in 1904 and the name was changed to Bergstrom Paper Company. They enlarged the building in order to install 132- and 158-foot paper machines, and then built another building to accommodate new finishing equipment. The John Strange Paper Company was among the first in the country to manufacture kraft wrapping paper in 1907, and was considered very progressive in 1917 when they installed a 144-foot cylinder machine, described at that time as the widest paper machine in the world. The Krueger and Lachmann Milling Company was the last of Neenah's once-flourishing flour mills to be converted to paper manufacturing. In 1918 it became the Neenah Paper Company.

In Neenah, as in other small towns, boys grew up and went on to college or, more likely, stayed at home to work with their fathers and brothers in the paper mills. It was through the efforts of Dr. J.E. Chapi that Neenah lads had an organized group of their own when the Boys Brigade was established in January 1900. The organization, patterned after its counterpart in Great Britain and similar groups on the

East Coast, signed 46 boys as charter members. The brigade, still in existence, celebrated its 84th birthday in January 1984. Yachting and sailing on Lake Winnebago has always been part of the enjoyment and advantage of living in Neenah and Menasha. Charles Doty had a sailboat as early as 1859 and within a few years Elbridge Smith and John Kimberly were sailing their own yachts. They cruised the lake, raced and sponsored regattas. The Neenah Yacht Club was organized in 1874 and was open to anyone with experience or an interest in sailing. By the 80s it was an upperclass social organization. Membership was expensive and so were yachts.

Charles B. Clark had a custom-built, sixty-three foot steam yacht that cost $5,000 in 1886. John Stevens owned a 100-foot vessel with a crew of professional seamen.

If C.B. "Bill" Clark had his way, Neenah would remain not only a fine place to raise children, but a "moral" city as well. Clark, a Yale University graduate, became a First Ward alderman in 1908. Four years later he was elected mayor of Neenah and assumed a personal challenge "to clean up the city." Although Neenah did not actually have a red light district, there were certain houses well know to "traveling men and local gentry of uncertain morals." Clark and the city council passed an ordinance "prohibiting the operation of houses of ill fame or leasing of premises therefor, or being of an inmate thereof, or detaining certain person therein." Clark then used his own money to hire a detective to compile enough evidence to quietly and methodically confront every such establishment. It was evident that the mayor was determined. There was a somewhat speedy exodus of red light business and Neenah's reputation as a "fine and moral place to live" was restored.

Every day brings big opportunities to the man with a Ford.

I'LL TAKE HER HOME FOR YOU!

Clark was the son of a self-made millionaire who was a mayor of Neenah, a member of the United States Assembly, and a Congressman. He died at the age of 47, when young Bill was just eight years old. The young boy never forgot that his father died at a friend's house in Theresa,

Three generations of the Wildenberg family operated this blacksmith and wagon-making shop in Little Chute.

New York because no hospital was available.

When Bill was a junior at Yale, his sister Theda died at her home in Neenah after the delivery of her first child. With the $96,000 his sister left the city, Bill Clark built a hospital. With the help and support of his wife, Jesse, Theda Clark hospital was started in 1909 and a School of Nursing in 1912. It was an act that would revolutionize health care in the valley. Classes were held at the hospital, Neenah High School and

Lawrence College in Appleton.

In 1911 Appleton exhibited its first "big cheese" at the National Dairy Show in Chicago. Four feet high and almost eight feet in diameter, the cheese weighted 12,360 pounds and was sold to a Chicago store. The first piece was cut and tested by President William Howard Taft. Within the next decade the Fox Cities would be the center of one of the wealthiest farm and livestock districts in Wisconsin. Dairying and cattle were the valleys protection

against a fluctuating economy in the beginning of the 20th century. As the century progressed and the paper industry flourished, the Fox Cities would find another source of protection against the economic depressions suffered in the 1920s.

Women as well as men welcomed the jobs and financial stability that the paper industry provided. More and more women were working in the mills and even attending college. Lawrence numbered a total of 31 women among its 52 graduates

in 1922.

There was at the same time a national movement opposing coeducation. Wardon Curtiss, a member of the movement at the University of Wisconsin, Madison, penned his feelings:

"I believe that the whole anti-coeducation movement rests upon the present-day competition of women with men. It has gone so far that men are driven out even of machine shops by women. The great crucial fact of today, for the future of the race lies in it, is that woman deprives man not merely of his former opportunities for employment, but of herself. The college girl is visibly preparing herself to compete with the college boy and to live without him. Misogyny is no mere college phenomenon. It is world-wide and woman is hated solely because more and more, man is prevented from loving her."

The anti-coeducation movement was undone by simple necessity with the assassination of Archduke Ferdinand, beginning the "war to end all wars".

The sinking of the passenger ship *Lusitania* brought the United States into the war against Imperial Germany in 1917. As men left to fight, labor in the valley became scarce and more dependent on female workers. Production boomed though products were modified in support of the war effort. Appleton Woolen Mills, for example, produced 123,000 "dough boy" blankets—some small relief for the misery and cold facing Fox Cities sons and brothers in the trenches of Europe. Outagamie County sacrificed 62 of her sons in World War I, and was honored in 1921 when Sergeant John E. Hantschel was selected by President Warren G. Harding to represent the state of Wisconsin at the Armistice Day public burial of the "Unknown Soldier" at Arlington National Cemetary in Washington, D.C.

The war's end brought a housing boom

to Appleton as veterans returned. In 1920 the Appleton Chamber of Commerce counted 2,800 home owners. That same year 175,000 tons of freight were carried by Fox River boats. With its 5,000 telephones, Appleton had the largest telephone switching office in Wisconsin, handling 30,000 local calls a day.

A retail price survey compiled by the Chamber in 1921 suggests that the high cost of living was a concern to valley residents. Ladies could buy a pair of silk hose for $1.50 in 1914 and paid $3.00 in 1921. Mens' bib overalls increased from $1.00 to $2.00. Car fare went up from 5¢ to 7¢, a shave from 15¢ to 25¢, and if you bought a daily newspaper it cost 10¢ a week in 1914 and 15¢ in 1921. Telephone service cost $1.25 per month in 1914 and $1.75 in 1921. If you called the doctor, he'd make a house call for $1.50, but by 1921 it had increased to $3.00. A 10¢ vaudeville ticket jumped to 40¢, and if you were in the eighth grade, your text book cost $2.15 in 1914 and a whopping $4.92 in 1921. The most dramatic increase was rent which spiraled 88 percent in those seven years.

Transportation in the area too underwent some rather dramatic changes during this era. The cities along the Fox River had begun as strategic locations for water transportation. Navigational hardships grew along with the increase in population and trade. Private companies built dams and locks and charged a toll. They were bought by the state who later sold the entire river project to The Green Bay-Mississippi Canal Company. With the Civil War came federal control of the Fox. More locks and dams were built and in tonnage the Fox was the second busiest river of its class in the country.

Railroads were at first regarded as welcome partners rather than competitors to waterways. If the rails could bring produce and products to the Mississippi and the Great Lakes for shipment by water, why wouldn't it work well too for the Fox and Wisconsin rivers? But with the advent of more and more railroads, it became evident that water transport was slower and more difficult. Rail facilities multiplied and provided continuous shipping for longer distances. Railroads lowered their rates during the navigation season and raised their fees when ice closed off many waterways. It became obvious that railroads were rivals rather than partners.

Neenah's first railroad was the Chicago and Northwestern, which was part of the

This Room Is Equipped With
Edison Electric Light.

Do not attempt to light with
match. Simply turn key
on wall by the door.

The use of Electricity for lighting is in no way harmful
to health, nor does it affect the soundness of sleep.

EARLY ELECTRIC SWITCHES,
INCANDESCENT BULBS, AND
FUSE

143

Beautiful and stately homes throughout the Fox Valley express the individuality and pride of their owners, as well as the heritage of the region. Hearthstone (right) was the first house in the nation to be lit with incandescent light. The Q.D. Marston home (opposite page, bottom) was built by a Civil War veteran. Photos (below right and opposite page, top) by Bill Van Den Brandt. Other photos courtesy, Outagamie County Historical Society, Inc.

The sign in the image reads:

WORLD'S FIRST
HYDROELECTRIC
CENTRAL STATION

Near this site on September 30, 1882, the world's first hydroelectric central station began operation. The station, here reproduced, was known as the Vulcan Street Plant and had a direct current generator capable of lighting 250 sixteen candle power lamps each equivalent to 50 watts. The generator operated at 110 volts and was driven through gears and belts by a water wheel operating under a ten foot fall of water.

*Above and above right
A replica of the Vulcan Street hydroelectric central station stands in Appleton today as an historic landmark. The first such station to have its own building, it was technically the nation's second Edison hydroelectric plant—the first had been in an Appleton pulp mill. Photos by Bill Van Den Brandt*

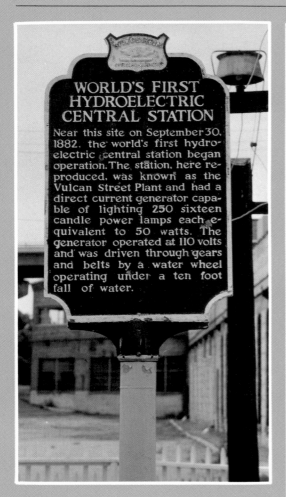

WORLD'S FIRST HYDROELECTRIC CENTRAL STATION

Near this site on September 30, 1882, the world's first hydro-electric central station began operation. The station, here reproduced, was known as the Vulcan Street Plant and had a direct current generator capable of lighting 250 sixteen candle power lamps each equivalent to 50 watts. The generator operated at 110 volts and was driven through gears and belts by a water wheel operating under a ten foot fall of water.

Right
Nowadays the Old Clock Tower at Neenah contrasts with much newer surroundings. The tower was preserved when the old City Hall was torn down. Photo by Bill Van Den Brandt

Above
A former Appleton High School student, John H. Bradley, was the second marine from the right in the famous Iwo Jima flag-raising of World War II.

Left
Erected in 1911, a statue of three soldiers at Soldiers' Square in Appleton pays tribute to "those who fought on land and sea to preserve under one flag the heritage of freedom bequeathed by our forefathers to their posterity." Photo by Bill Van Den Brandt

This street scene features
many elements of Appleton's
past, including Kresge's, the
old-style buses, and an ad for
Adler Brau Beer.

Above
Bicycle- and foot-races in the 1982 Festival of Light gave everyone a chance to "get physical." Such activities are popular throughout the Fox Valley.

Left
Cross-country skiers hit the snowy trails during the wintertime in the Fox Valley. Courtesy, Fox Cities Chamber of Commerce

A myriad of festivals and celebrations result in dazzling shows and parades and a wonderful spectrum of colors throughout the Fox Valley.

Clowns, balloons, and unusual
crafts abound at the annual
Octoberfest. Photos by Bill
Van Den Brandt

The headquarters of the Aid Association for Lutherans was moved from its downtown site and relocated just outside of Appleton. The AAL later reaffirmed its city ties and, in the late 1970s, moved some departments back into its downtown building. The AAL building is silhouetted in this dramatic sunset view. Photo by Image Studios, OCHS

protection, and in the feeling of spirit and pride that united the valley.

On June 14, 1946, the largest celebration Appleton had ever seen stretched from the College Avenue parade route all the way to Goodland Field, where General Carl A. Spaatz gave a "rousing patriotic speech", followed by a huge banquet and a military ball held at the Armory. Every community in the valley honored its war heroes in a similiar welcome-home celebration and every community mourned those lost.

POST WORLD WAR II

The post-war years brought major, sweeping changes to the Fox River Valley. Emphasis was on expansion, increased production and vast technological advancements. At the forefront of this progress was the paper industry, which became more aware of the need to protect and preserve natural resources and formed the Sulphite Pulp Manufacturers' Research League in 1939. Comprised of 13 of the state's paper companies, the league developed practical ways to improve paper-mill rivers by using or treating spent sulfite liquor. In the next 40 years the industry would spend more than $400 million in pollution controls. In 1950, paper industry leaders formed The Wisconsin Paper Council, a communications association of pulp and paper manufacturers, converters, and allied industries in the state. The council still serves as a center for the exchange of ideas, dissemination of information, and promotion of programs designed to create an understanding and awareness of the paper industry.

Other industries continued to push out their walls. There were more people, more children, and a need for more schools. Cities annexed land for new hospitals, businesses, churches, new roads and waterworks. H.C. Prange bought out the Pettibone Peabody Store in Appleton. The Aid Association for Lutherans climbed up past the Zuelke Building to become the tallest structure in the city. Wisconsin Avenue sacrificed all its trees in order to

widen the street, and the west end of College Avenue expanded to four lanes and extended to Highway 41.

Appleton became the third largest retail sales center in the state and matched the national average in home construction and population increase. With the constant flow of employment and services between the river cities, connections of every sort and kind tied the people of the Fox. In the years from 1950 to the mid-70s these connections would be solidified by the construction of a series of bridges between the Fox Cities.

In August, 1951, 5,000 people attended the formal dedication ceremonies for Menasha's new $606,000 Racine Street Bridge. Climaxing a 10-year wait and 19 months of construction, it replaced the 65-year-old Mill Street span. Delayed by World War II, contractor and railroad strikes, and steel shortages caused by the Korean War, the completion of the bridge symbolized a turning point, a growth mark in the Fox Cities. Life was beginning to move faster in an upward spiral of expansion and change.

Nowhere was this more evident than in industrial development. The J.W. Hewitt Machine Company enlarged its building and added roll grinding equipment, and the Banta Publishing Company built its Midway Plant between Menasha and Appleton. World War II veterans had little difficulty finding employment in the valley. The late '40s and early '50s building boom included a $90,000 addition at Neenah Paper Company, and expansion and remodeling at Neenah Foundry, Neenah Milk Products, Atlas Tag, and Bergstrom Paper. With war contracts completed, Kimberly-Clark remodeled its Kimlark plant into an engineering center and machine shops and converted its Neenah Mill into a research center.

Labor unions have always played an important part in the work history of Neenah-Menasha, and by the late 1950s, six thousand wage earners belonged to over 50 local unions. Neenah's first labor union was organized in 1882 when 15 iron workers at Bergstrom Foundry formed a local of the Molders and Foundry Workers Union. In 1894 Labor Day was declared a legal holiday and the valley's first Labor Day parade was held. 500 workers marched down Neenah's Wisconsin Avenue to Schuetzen Park for a Labor Day picnic. By 1900 iron molders, barbers, carpenters, masons and boot and shoe workers belonged to a five-union Central Labor Body.

An unsuccessful strike in the early 1900s by the papermakers at Kimberly-Clark may have been a turning point that discouraged union activity in valley mills for many years, according to historian Ebbe Berg. There were no strong national union organizations to provide financial backing, and the public was opposed to workers making demands on employers. When times were good, unions prospered, only to fall apart during lean years.

The Pulp, Sulphine and Paper Mill Workers organized in 1916, and it was then that the three-shift, eight-hour day was introduced for paper machine workers in the valley. When President Roosevelt's National Labor Relations Act became law union activity flourished in Neenah-Menasha, and from 1933 to 1957,

And Now...

With the decade of the '80s there is one word to apply to the cities and towns of the Fox River Valley—prosperous. But it is more than just economic prosperity that sets these communities apart from others. The difference lies in their extraordinarily high quality of life. According to MONEY magazine the Fox Cities is one of "the best of the small city breed economically and as an attractive place to work and live."

ENVIRONMENT

The 1980s has seen a rekindled interest in preserving and beautifying the Lower Fox River. Water and air pollution, hazardous and nuclear waste, pesticide control and wetlands preservation have been the big environmental issues in the valley in the 1980s. During the summer of 1981, Dr. William Sloey of the University of Wisconsin-Oshkosh monitored the quality of the water of Lake Winnebago and compared it to the same survey he did for the Fox Valley Water Quality Planning Agency in 1976. The news was good. The lake was responding to effective farm run-off control and point-source pollution control. Sloey's report showed nearly 40 percent less phosphorus in the lake in 1981, which resulted in nearly 50 percent less

algae. Cost-sharing programs were started to encourage farmers to work hard at "best management practices" in order to keep land nutrients out of the lakes and rivers.

Downtown Appleton had a new tenant in 1971 when a brand new Gimbels Department Store opened its doors to the public. The Aid Association for Lutherans, one of the largest fraternal insurance companies in the nation housed their home office in downtown Appleton, and in 1977 their staff of 1,200 moved into new headquarters three miles north of the city, off Highway 41. Continued growth led AAL to reopen its downtown office after a two-year vacancy.

With improvements in highways, the construction of many new bridges, the revitalization of downtown areas, and the immigration of new industry, the Fox Cities faced the approaching decade of the 80s from a position of strength. Bonds forged between communities in the early 20th century had been tempered in the heat of burgeoning growth to emerge in the 1970s as solid connections between the cities of the Fox.

An extensive monitoring program near the mouth of the Fox River and in the lower portion of the Bay of Green Bay during the summer of 1982 was the largest water quality study ever conducted in the Fox Valley. It was sponsored by the University of Wisconsin Sea Grant Program, the Green Bay Metropolitan Sewerage District, Department of Natural Resources several local industries, and the Fox Valley Water Quality Planning Agency. The report of that study highlighted the need for a uniform comprehensive state policy on wetlands. The Fox River flows as a "good news" river too. Before the early 1970s federal and state antipollution laws became effective, the river was considered one of the 10 most polluted rivers in the country. The lower Fox, a corridor of heavy industry between Appleton and Green Bay, reeked with industrial discharge and untreated sewage. Recent Department of Natural Resources reports show dramatic improvement in Wisconsin water quality over the past several years. The paper industry alone has spent $400 million on pollution abatement equipment. The cost to operate such equipment is $90 million a year or $25.82 for every ton of paper produced. In cooperation with area municipal dischargers, paper mills on the Fox and Wisconsin rivers take daily readings of the river's flow rate and temperature levels, making it possible for daily operational adjustments to meet the changing assimilative capacity of the rivers.

And now that pollution has been sharply reduced, there's a simpler way to measure the water quality of the Fox River. Even though the river bottom still contains chemical sediments, walleyes, perch, white bass, and smelt are running,

and anglers are fishing the river again.

The high cost of maintaining the lock system on the Fox River, however, defied an easy solution in the '80s. An information-gathering Governor's Task Force pondered future funding and operation of the 17 locks between DePere and Menasha. Options, to keep the locks open, include making the locks part of the park system, instituting boater user fees or state gasoline tax money collected from boaters. A grant of $900,000 enabled the locks to operate through the 1984 boating season, but without state, local, or private funding sources, the storied locks may be doomed.

The continuing preservation of one of the oldest houses in the valley was assured in 1981 when the Outagamie County Historical Society acquired the historical collection, grounds and house built by Charles A. Grignon in 1838. In 1980 the Fox Cities Arts Alliance was organized to promote community awareness, appreciation and coordination of the arts, and to exchange ideas and plans among Fox Cities arts groups and artists.

Long considered a sports-minded area, the valley offers eight public and five private golf courses. Local park and recreation programs include softball, touch football, basketball, volleyball and ice hockey leagues. Two YMCAs and several health clubs and sports centers offer handball, racketball, swimming, and health and fitness classes. Indoor tennis and indoor skating and hockey are available, as are all-season outdoor activities in the area's excellent system of parks and recreational facilities.

The Appleton Foxes, a Class A Midwest League baseball farm team of the Chicago White Sox, provide the opportunity to follow the fortunes of professional athletes, as do the Green Bay Packers.

When a group of local businessmen sponsored Appleton's first Red Smith Sports Dinner in 1965, its main purpose was to raise funds for local sports and athletic programs. Little did they know the idea would catch fire, become an annual sell-out banquet attracting some of the top names in the sports world, and provide thousands of dollars for local athletes. Appleton hosted its 19th annual banquet in 1984, and gave the prestigious Red Smith Award to the Green Bay Packers' Jan Stenerud, who has kicked more field goals than anyone in pro football history.

With its proud history in the heart of the world's heaviest concentration of papermaking activity, perhaps the Fox River Valley can be defined as a giant, a paper giant. The socioeconomic impact of the industry on the area is certainly significant. The pulp and paper industry in the 1980s accounts for 35 percent of the valley employment and 40 percent of its income.

Paper industry executives who were interviewed by the Post-Crescent's business and labor editor, Arlin Boardman, for the paper's 1983 progress edition, expressed caution and optimism as they looked to the future. The Fox River Valley followed the trends of the nation as the recession that began in the mid-1970s forced the paper industry to juggle high inventories and collapsing demand for paper products. The year 1982 "was a slow but satisfactory year from the standpoint of the overall economy and we held our own", said John Hangen, chairman of the board and chief executive officer of Appleton Papers, Inc. Wisconsin Tissue Mills started an $82 million expansion program just as the recession hit. "The tissue industry (napkins, towels, toilet tissues, etc.) experienced a four percent average annual compounded growth rate from 1975 to 1982, but Wisconsin Tissue more than doubled that rate," according to James Asmuth, president and chief executive officer. The mill's expansion was the most ambitious ever and Asmuth expected their operating rate to reach slightly over 90 percent in 1984. Darwin Smith, chairman of the board and chief executive officer of Kimberly-Clark, in his advance 1982 report said their tissue machines ran near capacity levels for the year. They announced expansion plans for a new 430,000-square-foot Huggies diaper

plant in Texas and a multi-million-dollar nonwoven production facility in Georgia. The Bergstrom Division of P.H. Glatfelter Company uses recycled fiber for printing and writing paper, and for computer printout paper. D.W. Bergstrom, division president said "1981 and 1982 were excellent years," and attributed it to their product mix, depressed pulp prices, and long-time, loyal customers. Bergstrom anticipates the recycled fiber industry to grow substantially in the 1980s and 1990s.

But the recessionary gloom in the Fox Valley left some residents without jobs. Neenah Foundry Company reduced their inventory with production cutbacks and temporary layoffs. Wisconsin Tissue Mills and Menasha Paperboard Mill had to lay off some of their employees. By October 1980 the state department of Industry, Labor and Human Relations listed the Appleton to Oshkosh area unemployment rate at 8.4 percent. Unemployment remained erratic in 1982 and 1983 as Consolidated Papers-Appleton Division closed its doors in 1982 and put 173 out of work. When national and world-wide orders slacked off, Miller Electric Manufacturing used a combination of layoffs, and shutdowns to cut back on production. Foundries, farm equipment companies, and the construction business were also hard hit. Despite problems with the economy and the fluctuating uncertainties of the past few years, optimism runs high. When asked about the long-range forecast, Thomas Schmidt of the Wisconsin Paper Council pictures the paper industry as "progressive, with forward-thinking management. Firms in the valley and the state have been in a constant state of rebuilding, modernizing and expanding. Since 1980, they've invested more than $450 million in capital projects designed to expand or upgrade their operations." Kenneth E. Lowe, director of communications and information services, Paper Industry Forecasts, predicts the national and paper industry economic outlook for 1983 through 1992 as a "period of modest growth and aggressive competition compared with previous economic eras. Manufacturing capacity should expand 1.3 percent yearly and capital spending may well reach $16 billion by 1992."

In 1982, the valley commemorated the centennial of Edison hydroelectricity in America with a four-day "Festival of Light" celebration. For five cents, you could ride a newly restored, vintage electric streetcar powered by hydroelectricity. The "River Queen," a sternwheel flat bottom riverboat, provided rides on the Fox River. There was an "Electric 80s Ball" in the Grand Ballroom of the new Paper Valley Hotel, a variety of exhibits, a Thomas Edison look-alike contest, and a night-time "Light" parade. There were bicycle races, a Kermis Dutch Fall Festival in Little Chute, Dancing Waters-Lazer Light Show, Venetian Boat Parade at Jefferson Park in Menasha, and a huge fireworks display as a grand finale for the valley's 100-year birthday party celebrating hydroelectricity and American inventiveness.

APPLETON

According to a 1975 national survey by the Midwest Research Institute of Kansas City, Appleton ranked third in the nation's cities for its quality of life. Locally,

Lawrence University Survey Research Center, under the direction of William Markam, Assistant Professor of Sociology, conducted attitudinal surveys of Appleton residents in 1977, 1978, and 1980. Markham said, "Almost every indicator of socio-economic status or prosperity one could examine shows that Appleton is far better off than the nation as a whole."

The surveys showed 60 percent of Appleton's workforce as white-collar, as compared to 48 percent nationwide. Twenty-five percent of the households surveyed had family incomes over $25,000 against 15 percent nationally and only one-fourth had incomes below $10,000. Seventy-five percent owned their own homes, and 98 percent of those interviewed owned a car. Only 18 percent of the interviewees had less than a high school education, compared with 37 percent nationwide, and 23 percent had a college degree versus 14 percent nationally. Ninety-eight percent of those interviewed felt Appleton was a good place to live, listing shopping, health care, housing and entertainment as the major reasons. Seven percent said Appleton was virtually problem-free, and only three percent worried that crime affected the quality of life in their city.

Downtown Appleton is an urban area that has survived the economic challenge of additional retail centers in suburban areas. In the spring 1980 issue of *Lawrence Today*, William Brehm, Jr., Director of Planning and Development, said, "A great amount of community pride and satisfaction in Appleton exists among its residents. A central theme is a pride in the downtown. There is an almost emotional love of College Avenue."

In recent years, Appleton has managed to maintain that love and pride while making room for the new. The familiar red sandstone city hall is gone with a striking new library in its place. The Congregational Church on Lawrence Street has made way for the high rise Skyline Bridge. A new post office replaces the old, and the Conway Hotel has been converted to apartments for the elderly.

Two-term mayor James Sutherland was defeated by a "time for a change" campaign when Appleton elected their 35th chief executive in 1980. Dorothy Johnson, the first woman ever elected to head the city, faced an immediate need for a strong downtown redevelopment plan. A major step was taken toward this redevelopment when the city accepted a proposal from Neenah businessman John Bergstrom for a downtown hotel convention center. The 194-room Paper Valley Hotel and Conference Center has attracted a number of new visitors to the area since its opening in June 1982.

Music, dance, theatre and art are alive and well in Appleton. With its roots at Lawrence University, a population of 60,000 plus, and the largest city in the area, the city asserts itself as the cultural center of the valley. Schools, university and college campuses provide concerts, lectures and film series.

From the strongly supported Fox Valley Symphony to the orchestras, jazz ensemble and concert groups at Lawrence; from children's choirs to barbershop and Sweet Adelines, much of the voice of the valley is musical. And as much as its residents love music, they flock in even greater numbers to anything theatrical. The Lawrence University Music-Drama Center has three public auditoriums, a recital hall, 300-seat theatre, and a 500-seat, proscenium-type theatre. Pickard Auditorium at Armstrong High School in Neenah seats 1,600, and Appleton High School West's remodeled theatre, 1,400 people. There are eight theatre groups, including two for children. The Lawrence Community Artist Series and the Lectures and Fine Arts Series of the University of Wisconsin Center-Fox Valley bring well-known performers and speakers to the area.

That Appletonians identify proudly with their landscape, their traditions, their mutual sense of community is evident in the hundreds of volunteers and thousands of people who line the streets for the annual Flag Day Parade (the only one of its kind in the nation) and the Christmas Parade and "Octoberfest." Closing off College Avenue in downtown Appleton to make room for ethnic food and craft booths, sound stages, bands, and a variety of entertainment, "Octoberfest" attracted an estimated 100,000 people in 1983.

KAUKAUNA

Kaukauna, one of the oldest communities in the valley, has also been called "The Friendly City" and "Electric City." The Fox River, with its 50 foot drop within the boundaries of the city, generates electrical power from five plants. Kaukauna's municipally-owned electric utility offers one of the lowest electrical rates in Wisconsin, and also provides service to Little Chute and part of Combined Locks.

Thilmany Pulp and Paper Company, a division of Hammermill Paper Company, Erie, Pennsylvania, is the largest employer and is nationally recognized for its packaging and paper specialty lines. Other significant Kaukauna employers include Roloff Manufacturing, Giddings and Lewis, and Badger Northland.

Revitalization of downtown Kaukauna began in October, 1980. A Downtown Improvement Committee was formed to work hand-in-hand with the East Central Wisconsin Regional Planning Commission to establish a 12-month rejuvenation plan. The '80s also brought a $350,000 federal Community Development Block Grant for low-income and elderly housing, and new quarters for the Heart of the Valley Chamber of Commerce, which represents 13 communities from Appleton to DePere.

Improvement of the city's fiscal situation and downtown revitalization continue as Kaukauna's two most important issues in the '80s, according to Kaukauna Mayor Robert Van De Hey. Quoted in the December 2, 1983, issue of the *Appleton Post Crescent*, Van De Hey said, "The people in the community feel good about themselves and you can sense the civic pride. You can walk down the street and talk to people and to the merchants and

Appleton is regionally famous for its annual Flag Day parade featuring more than 100 units. This 1982 parade is shown turning from State Street onto West College Avenue. Post-Crescent *photo, OCHS*

see it, hear it and feel it."

LITTLE CHUTE

To ensure continuous development, the Little Chute Village Board embraced a 10-year Community Development Plan in 1980. With the help of the East Central Wisconsin Regional Planning Commission, the program included adding a full time village administrator, improving traffic patterns and business area parking, well-planned annexation, and improving Heesakker's Woods for additional park facilities.

In 1983 the village was divided into nine wards and three voting districts, eliminating the one central voting site at the Village Hall. Community spirit runs deep and Little Chute may be the only community in the nation with its own "village anthem." Three churches, two of which maintain their own parochial school, provide for the spiritual needs of the

people of predominately Dutch heritage. The new shelter at Doyle Park and special air packs for the Little Chute fire department are just two examples of the public service acts that are not at all unusual in this growing community.

The population of Little Chute climbed from 5,522 in 1970 to 8,339 in 1982. Tagged "the fastest growing community, residential-wise, in the heart of the valley," Little Chute has experienced a 10-year housing boom. Although there was a national housing recession in 1980, in Little Chute many new homes were being built and purchased.

COMBINED LOCKS

From its beginning as a mill town, the village of Combined Locks has always been linked to the paper industry. The paper mill, now operated by Appleton Papers, Inc. and a subsidiary of BATUS Inc. of London, England, has an average

In a 1948 aerial view, the village of Kimberly is dominated by the river-front Kimberly Mill on the site of the Smithfield Methodist mission to the Oneida Indians. Across the river (to the extreme left) is the location where the signing of the Treaty of the Cedars took place. In the background stretches the predominantly Dutch village of Little Chute. Today the Kimberly Mill is operated by Midtec Paper Company. SHSW

employment of 650 and continues to provide a strong economic base for Combined Locks. Through the years, the paper mill has donated land and money for projects and betterment of the community. With a population of 2,508, Combined Locks is the smallest of the Fox Cities, but boasts most of the major services of its neighboring communities.

A large percent of the mostly Dutch residents of the village are Catholic and St. Paul is the only church in Combined Locks. The community is proud of its extensive park system and has designated a wooded ravine area as a conservancy zone to preserve its natural state for future generations.

Combined Locks has been described by local residents as "suburban living at its best. It's a quiet place to live, where everyone knows their neighbor and lends a helping hand in time of need."

KIMBERLY

Kimberly, with its tree-lined streets and well-kept homes, is the second smallest community in the valley. With a population of 5,947, it is one of the few villages of its size to support its own library. Its park system is an enviable one, consisting of more than 50 acres.

Midtec Paper Corporation, located on the site of the first Oneida Indian mission on the Fox River in 1822, is responsible for the village's solid economy. The company, which produces book, machine coated book paper and other specialty papers, is the village's largest employer.

Due to a healthy respect for long-range planning, Kimberly is considered both a progressive and prosperous community. Although building construction dropped considerably in the early 1980s, few people noticed as the topic of conversation was the $70 million "Gingerbell," a new paper machine at Midtec Paper. The machine meant continuing employment for Fox Valley residents, the capability of doubling production, and an even sounder tax base for Kimberly. In a Chamber of Commerce booklet, highlighting the communities

within the Fox River Valley, Kimberly is described as "an ideal place to live, a picturesque, modern community with hardy, industrious citizens who have strong community pride and who are willing to work together in maintaining its history of growth and prosperity."

NEENAH AND MENASHA

The League of Women Voters of Neenah-Menasha, in their 1981 revised edition of "A Tale of Two Cities and Four Towns," paints Neenah and Menasha as a

"blend of town and country, a study in contrasts. Industries include both national and international giants in the fields of paper, printing, packaging and metal casting, yet ten minutes to the South or West is prime Wisconsin farmland, rich and productive. The waterways offer year-round recreational activities and beauty in all seasons, but they are working waters too, and historically have drawn industries rather than tourists. Thom Ciske's promise to run city government like a business proved effective in the 1982 mayoral election and downtown redevelopment became a top priority. Determined to breathe life into Menasha's core area, Ciske explained his point of view to the *Northwestern* newspaper in January 1983:

> *The days of a large department store coming into a downtown and increasing shopper traffic is over. Major retailers now want the people there first. I think our first step should be to try to get office*

_buildings downtown. When shopper
traffic picks up because of this, then
the businesses will come._

A 42-year-old millworker who has lived
in Menasha all his life says,

_"We're kind of a small town with a
personality as pleasing as a cool glass
of beer. But people go other places to
shop. Everything we've tried for_

_downtown has failed. But we're used
to fighting for what we believe in.
We'll find a way to bring it back, just
wait and see. Menasha won't die."_

Neenah, with its dozens of decorative old
Victorian homes, hundreds of sailboats in
the harbor, the Bergstrom Art Center and
Mahler Glass Museum, old clock tower,
and new auditorium, has a "dress up", a
cultured look. Despite this seeming
sophistication, Neenah is just as well
known for its dozens of parks and its
feeling of "home townness."

Neenah came at their downtown
redevelopment problem from a different
angle. Viewed by some as a pioneering
effort, The Future Neenah Committee was
formed in 1982. A mixture of private,
public and political leaders, whose goal it is
to revitalize downtown, has raised funds,
involved downtown merchants, elicited
community support, and hired the services
of an East Coast development consulting
firm. Downtown Neenah plans to have a
new look by the mid-1980s, making it a
competitive and energetic center for
shopping, entertainment, offices and
housing.

Neenah-Menasha has already experienced
some outstanding growth in the '80s.
Neenah's Theda Clark Regional Center
began performing open-heart surgery in
1981. A $10 million expansion project is
also underway to centralize inventory,
purchasing, storing, distribution of supplies,
and a computer system.

The $1.7 million Breezewood-Bell
overpass in Neenah designed to provide a
rail-free, east-west route through the city is
considered an enhancement to the
industrial park located south of Bell Street
and next to Highway 41.

Marigen Carpenter, a former
alderwoman, and president of the common
council, was triumphant in her bid to
become Neenah's first woman mayor in
1982. She went to work immediately
authoring the first executive city budget,
eliminating residency requirements for city
employees, and encouraging the purchase

of the 168-acre Kampo property for $1 million to create an industrial park on Neenah's southwest side.

In an early 1983 interview, Mayor Carpenter told Bill Schultz of the *Northwestern*,

> *"More than ever before, we're realizing that what the future of the city is, is in our own hands. With diminishing state and federal financial aids, the city must choose its own direction in the future and rely on its own resources. I've always felt that Neenah has a great deal going for it. The city is in sound financial condition, has a high quality of life, and potential for improvement."*

THE TWIN CITIES

It is not unusual or surprising that Neenah and Menasha face some of the same problems. From the beginning they could easily have been one city. Instead they became rival communities, nurturing their differences for well over a century. From the first land and money bickerings of Harrison Reed and Harvey Jones, the Twin Cities were at odds with one another over the building of canals and railways. Inhabitants took sides and kept careful tabs on what was happening on the other side of the river. Traditionally, Menasha voted Democratic and Neenah Republican. Menasha was known as the working man's town, while in the early years, millowners settled in Neenah.

The two cities argued over everything, from who would pay for jointly-ordered streetlights to which street cleaner swept dirt from one side of the street into the other city. Boundary-line fist fights were common, and even newspapers insulted each other and rival officials, and boasted of their own city's athletic prowess. Ironically enough, for many years the annual Neenah-Menasha football game was played on Armistice Day as the last game of the season. Police in both cities had to employ a full crew to handle group fights, student invasions of either city, vandalism,

and when nothing else worked, they barricaded street and railway bridges to isolate each city.

Over the years the rivalry diminished. The Twin Cities grew up, expanded and matured. As one elderly resident put it, "We've lived in each other's pockets for so many years and it gets to be a tight fit once in awhile. There's bound to be a disagreement now and then, maybe even an explosion or two. But we have a lot more in common than we do in differences."

EPILOGUE

So how do you best describe the valley? Perhaps you start and end with the river where memories and traditions still cling like moss. Old Father Fox, a bit tired now, twists and winds his way through the very soul of the valley. And for every mile, for every bend, there are legends and stories as old as the Grignon house, the Doty cabin, the old weathered buildings that stand like sentinels in Appleton's industrial "flats." The Fox became a first highway, cradled and nurtured the early settlers and became one of the most likeliest places in the world to build a paper mill. Few rivers anywhere have etched a more enduring history.

Maybe the valley should be portrayed by its people. The people for whom the Fox became a handy waterway, who cherished a close bond, who learned to mesh their movements with the river's. The Indians, Jesuits, explorers. The fur traders, settlers, and farmers. Today, the valley has become a home-seeking refuge for Vietnamese and Hmong people from Laos with the largest concentration of Hmong refugees in Wisconsin.

For all their individuality and differences, Fox Citians live and think in terms of "community." The common heritage of uniqueness and pride, stability and success give each village, each city, an insistent feeling that they, all together, are the Fox River Valley. That sense of community that has cast the shape of the valley continues and is worth preserving.

The Hmong are the latest arrivals in a long history of ethnic pioneers to the Fox Valley. Post-Crescent *photo, OCHS*

179

Partners in Progress

It seems that the Fox River has always flowed through the economic veins of the wooded region of northeastern Wisconsin that eventually would become the Fox Cities.

It was home to the Native Americans and to the early trappers and traders, and a highway of commerce, the source of the supply and the demand for them.

Commerce first depended on it, for the fur traders and early settlers would not have had business to conduct without it.

Then there were the people who came to push seeds into the rich soil that the river's watershed created or to graze fat dairy cattle on the lush land. Theirs was the business of growing things, and for them the river was the primary link with the rest of the world. It made what was remote less remote, like living in a modern suburb but near a superhighway.

The area grew, developing its own commerce, and the enterprising businessmen who came to the area quickly saw that the Fox had still more to offer. It had the muscle to power the region's early industry.

It turned lumber mills, then flour mills, but perhaps most important, it turned paper mills, and paper making became central to the economy of the Fox Cities, forming a financial foundation that was almost unshakable, emerging virtually untouched by what had been hard economic times elsewhere.

The river also carried in its relentless flow another kind of power, something new and intriguing, and the youthful Fox Cities became the first place in the nation where a river was used to turn a hydroelectric generator and illuminate private homes. It was barely days after Thomas Edison put his first power company into business.

As the river itself drew commerce and industry, so did that commerce and industry itself draw, bringing industry associated with papermaking, from those who serviced this manufacturing at its head end with machinery and repairs, to those whose raw material was the paper, the converters and printers and packagers.

And thus the community that was to become the Fox Cities grew, building first on the economic footing of the river and then on its own strength.

This engraving shows downtown Neenah in 1880, looking west on Wisconsin Avenue. SHSW

FOX CITIES CHAMBER OF COMMERCE AND INDUSTRY

The Fox Cities Chamber of Commerce and Industry is the result of a marriage of two business organizations that each trace their history back more than 100 years. Those original groups were the Appleton Chamber of Commerce and the Chamber of Commerce of Neenah-Menasha.

The earliest recorded Appleton Chamber was formed in September 1874, with 20 members signing the constitution. The first president was Augustus Ledyard Smith, a mayor of the young city and a founder of the First National Bank.

In 1875 cotton growing was attempted in Outagamie County, and the Chamber campaigned to establish a cotton mill in the city. The project was dropped when cotton proved to be an unsuitable crop for the climate of northeastern Wisconsin.

The Chamber resurfaced in 1891 and again in 1892, and it was

The Fox Cities Chamber of Commerce and Industry's offices are located at 227 South Walnut Street, Appleton (above), and at 330 North Commercial Street, Neenah.

Today's Chamber was formed through a consolidation of the Chambers of Commerce of Appleton and Neenah-Menasha to more ably represent the interests of the Fox Cities.

reorganized still another time, amid much fanfare, in 1920, when 612 men became members in one day. W.C. Wing was its first chairman.

Unfortunately, little is known of the early history of the Chamber of Commerce of Neenah-Menasha, except that it, too, traces its history back more than 100 years and that it dates to separate organizations for each of the two communities.

The most significant date in the history of either organization is August 1, 1976. It was on this occasion that the two organizations consolidated to become the Fox Cities Chamber of Commerce and Industry, thereby creating both a broader geographical service base and a broader range of business interests.

Consolidating and broadening the two organizations meant recognition of more than changes in name and service area, however. It

acknowledged that there are common interests between commerce and industry and that there are even greater common interests among the separate communities of the Fox Cities.

At the time, the Appleton Area Chamber of Commerce had 749 members, and the Chamber of Commerce of Neenah-Menasha had 210.

John Bergstrom of Neenah was elected president of the newly formed Chamber, which made its headquarters in what had been the offices of the Appleton group. Donald Stone became executive vice-president of the new organization, a post he had held in the Appleton Chamber.

World War I.

Appleton Woolen Mills began to outgrow its facilities, with no possibility of expansion at its original location. Through the efforts of F. Harwood Orbison, who joined the firm in 1953 as general manager and was elected president in 1956, the old Outagamie County Airport was annexed to and purchased by the City of Appleton. Ground was broken in 1968, and Appleton Woolen Mills became the first industry to build in the new Northeast Industrial Park.

As synthetics began to replace wool in wet felts, the company deleted the word "woolen" from its name and in 1961 officially became "Appleton Mills."

F. Harwood Orbison died in 1980, and for the first time in 104 years there was neither a Harwood nor an

December 1961. Employees gather for the annual distribution of Christmas turkeys, a tradition followed every year since 1881.

Appleton Mills, 1983. The 190,000-square-foot headquarters building houses the finest production equipment in the world to manufacture top-quality papermakers' wet felts. All offices and a research and development complex are also contained within the facility.

Orbison at the helm. Orbison's grandfather, Frank J. Harwood of Ripon, Wisconsin, joined the venture as a partner in 1876 and became president in 1923. Orbison's great-grandfather, A.P. Harwood, had been incorporating president in 1881. A great-uncle, D.V.N. Harwood, was secretary/treasurer from 1883 to 1925. Orbison's father, T.E. "Gene" Orbison, son-in-law of Frank Harwood, managed engineering from

1935 to 1959, and when F.J. Harwood died in 1940, Orbison's mother, Ann Harwood Orbison, became president until her son assumed that duty in 1956.

Charles P. Heeter, vice-president and treasurer and an employee since 1949, was elected president and treasurer in 1980. He added a 22,080-square-foot expansion to the building in 1982, purchased more equipment, and expanded the staff.

Dramatic growth in the 1970s prompted offers to purchase, and on June 23, 1983, it was announced that Appleton Mills had been sold to Voith GmbH of Heidenheim, West Germany, an international giant owning many large companies, several in paper-related industries.

Appleton Mills' 190,000-square-foot headquarters building on a 31-acre site houses all offices and production facilities. It employs 240 persons, including salesmen across the United States and in Canada, Australia, and New Zealand.

GEORGE BANTA COMPANY, INC.

It seems almost inevitable that George Banta Company, Inc., should have come into being.

George Banta, Sr., had a fascination for printing that dated to his boyhood in Franklin, Indiana. There he haunted the newspaper printshop, scouring floor sweepings for odd pieces of type. He used these to print his first publication, *The Sun*, a newspaper whose name he chose because it was the only one he could spell with the heading type he had collected. Banta had no press, but inked the type and forced paper against it with the heel of his hand.

In his teens, with six dollars he had saved and five contributed by his

for Indiana and later Wisconsin, and when his young wife died of white plague, he moved to Wisconsin.

Here he met and married Ellen Lee Pleasants in 1886, and the couple established permanent residence and headquarters for the insurance business in Menasha.

But housekeeping with George Banta meant that Mrs. Banta had a dining room furnished with a printing press. When a second press taxed the tranquility of the household, again his avocation was relegated to a backyard woodshed. There Banta added more equipment and hired a full-time printer to help with his hobby.

Then, in 1901, the printshop was

Banta has enjoyed a close association with education. For many years it was known as "the Collegiate Press," which still appears on this bronze plaque at the entrance to the Menasha headquarters.

Banta pioneered the use of web-offset printing, now the predominant method in the industry, for book production. The company's first such press, purchased in 1940, has long been retired to this glass enclosure at the Midway Plant.

mother, Banta bought his first press, a small, hand machine, and set up shop in a woodshed.

He graduated from Indiana University in 1876 at the age of 19, but being more salesman than the barrister he had been expected to become, he joined the Phenix Insurance Co. as a field man.

After a time, he was given agencies

struck by fire, a disaster that turned to good fortune. So severe was the damage that the printing equipment, to protect it from the elements, had to be moved to a store building on Main Street in Menasha.

In that store Banta and his printer pursued his hobby, turning out insurance-business printings in what were intended to be temporary quarters. But, because of its business location, people began to ask to have job printing done there. Banta told his printer to accept, and the avocation turned into a vocation.

From that point on the company grew steadily. In 1910 the first plant

was built at the site of its present headquarters, at Curtis Reed Plaza in Menasha.

There was another milestone in 1929, when the firm printed its first elementary-school workbook. This was a brand-new educational tool then. Now Banta is a leading supplier of workbooks and other educational materials such as tests and multimedia kits.

Banta in 1946 began construction of its Midway Plant in Menasha. Numerous expansions have produced a facility covering nearly 13 acres—America's largest single book-manufacturing operation under one roof.

Banta began an aggressive expansion program in 1969, and by 1970 had acquired Daniels Manufacturing Co. (later Daniels Packaging), Rhinelander, Wisconsin;

This is the original building, around 1910, which was located on the site of the present corporate headquarters.

page assembly at Northwestern Color-graphics and Color Response, merchandising graphics by KCS Industries, and serves a growing catalog printing business.

Banta also has been important to the people of the Fox Cities, not only through the jobs it has provided, but also via the Banta Company Foundation, established in 1953 to provide financial aid to community projects, particularly those related to health care, education, history, and religion. Among these are Calder Stadium in Menasha, the Menasha Public Library, Lawrence University's Banta Bowl in Appleton, and High Cliff State Park.

And meanwhile, that little hand press that George Banta and his mother invested in so long ago rests in the company's library while multimillion-dollar presses whir nearby. And it still works.

Hart Press, Long Prairie, Minnesota; and Northwestern Engraving (later Northwestern Colorgraphics), Menasha. In 1973 Banta acquired Ling Packaging (later Ling Products) of Neenah, and in 1975, KCS Industries Inc. of Milwaukee. R.J. Carroll, Inc. (later Banta Company, Inc.-Harrisonburg), Harrisonburg, Virginia, was added in 1976, and Clark Printing Co., North Kansas City, Missouri, in 1981. The ninth Banta company, Color Response, Inc., was formed in Charlotte, North Carolina, in 1981.

Nationwide, Banta employs nearly 2,000 people serving four major market areas. Elementary and high school books, in addition to workbooks and learning kits, continue to be a mainstay, along with college texts and consumer books. Banta is a force in flexible packaging, with

Daniels primarily involved in the packaging of consumer products and Ling in the conversion of paper and polyethylene film to food-service and health-care products. Banta companies print about 200 magazines, with topics ranging from religion to business to hobbies. Finally, through its commercial graphic services segment, Banta provides prepress film services such as color separations and

In 1906 Banta was in the Masonic Building on Main Street in Menasha and was a going concern in "the business of job and newspaper printing, bookbinding, and manufacture of books and pamphlets," as its articles of incorporation stated.

FOX RIVER PAPER COMPANY
Division of Fox Valley Corporation

Captain G.W. Spaulding, who had been master and owner of clipper ships, left retirement on a Massachusetts farm to come to Appleton in 1858. Amos Lawrence, founder of Lawrence College in Appleton, had told him of the Fox River, its power and potential.

Spaulding ventured into a number of businesses—a sawmill and barrel-and-stave company among them—before he and other investors in 1883 founded Fox River Flour and Paper Company. Seeing the possible growth for paper and the fading future in milling, Spaulding, the first president of Fox River, soon dropped the flour portion of the business and concentrated on paper.

Within a few years, the firm and its 80-man mill were producing four tons of book and school paper a day. That first mill, known as the Ravine Mill, soon became too small, and a second building was constructed, boosting capacity to 12 tons a day. By the turn of the century, Fox River had capital stock of $.5 million.

Soon the company began making fine, watermarked bond paper, the first Midwest mill to do so. This was just one in a long line of "firsts" for Fox River. It was the first mill in the Midwest to install a mechanical loft to dry paper; the first to manufacture paper from cotton linters, which had been waste in the cotton industry; the first to add optical brighteners to its pulp; the first able to custom watermark paper off the machine; and the first to use the Swedish Flakt dryer.

By the early 1960s, however, Fox River had fallen on difficult times, and a local industrialist, William

Buchanan, Sr., bought the business. He wanted the longtime Fox Cities fixture to continue to operate.

The purchase generated an expansion that continued under William's son Robert, president and chief executive of the parent Fox Valley Corporation. In 1976 Fox River purchased the Eagle-A paper line from the Brown Company and in 1981 acquired the entire Plover line.

Since the Buchanan family purchased Fox River Company, shareholders have never received a dividend, reinvesting profits in the business. Fox River's share of the fine-paper market has increased dramatically. At the time of its centennial in 1983, production was up 65 percent and employment up 22 percent in six years.

Fox River had earned its reputation as an organization that defies extinction.

An early view of the firm, in 1883, when it was known as the Fox River Flour and Paper Company.

The present headquarters of Fox River Paper Company, which celebrated its centennial in 1983.

ARTFAIRE
Division of Fox Valley Corporation

Asa Frank Tuttle, founder of the Tuttle Press Company which was a forerunner of Artfaire. Photo circa 1930.

The world's first paper napkin was produced by Asa Frank Tuttle for the Chicago Fourth of July celebration in 1898.

Asa Frank Tuttle had a small printing plant in Elgin, Illinois, in 1898, and an idea that would become a part of everyday American life.

Tuttle had paper left over from an order for peach wrappers. He printed the American and Cuban flags on large squares of this tissue paper and quickly sold his product to a patriotic public celebrating victories of the Spanish-American War.

He had manufactured America's first paper napkin. It was so successful that he followed with a printing of another 10,000 bearing the likeness of Commodore Dewey, the hero of Manila. Orders increased rapidly, with many coming from such companies as Coca-Cola and Armour Beef, with their advertisements printed on the napkins.

Then, in 1902, at the urging of Wisconsin Tissue Mills, which supplied most of Tuttle's stock, he moved his operation to Appleton, eliminating the need to wait for shipment of stock and the high cost of transportation. The Hancock Street plant, still in use, was built in 1905.

Expansion was inevitable. Tuttle began making gift wrap of the same tissue, and a coordinated line of party goods evolved. At first, there were only simple, two-color designs. Then an artist was hired and more elaborate presses installed.

Tuttle was the first company to offer gift wrap in rolls, embossed coasters and napkins, flame-resistant crepe, and shingled packages. Product categories began to include bottle caps, tomato wrappers, liquor labels, decorated bags, and even toilet paper.

The firm broke ground for its Perkins Street Plant in 1963. It housed napkin and table-cover presses, while the Hancock Street plant printed and finished gift wrap.

The Artfaire Division of Fox Valley Corporation was created in 1983 through the merger of two former corporate divisions, Tuttle Press and the George S. Carrington Company of Leominster, Massachusetts.

This allowed the organization to broaden its line to include gift wrap, crepe paper, tablecloths, plates, cups, plastic tableware, cutouts, tags, labels, bows—and printed napkins.

OSCAR J. BOLDT CONSTRUCTION CO.

This was Martin Boldt's carpentry shop before 1900. Columns and cabinets were among the shop's specialties.

The crew of Martin Boldt & Sons poses on a scaffold during the 1920s.

It was in 1889 that Martin Boldt, an industrious carpenter of German parentage, founded what has become the largest construction company in Wisconsin.

Martin was a cabinetmaker, and as his business in Appleton grew and matured, he established a reputation for craftsmanship and reliability. He had three sons, Arthur, Robert, and Oscar J., each of whom left his mark on the venture. Martin Boldt became Martin Boldt & Sons, then the Oscar J. Boldt Construction Co.

Oscar J. was full of ideas and energy. He knew the value of good equipment and the sacrifices necessary to have it. He lacked the capacity to acknowledge defeat, a trait that has served the firm well through depressions and hard times.

Oscar J.'s son, Oscar C., built on the traditions of his grandfather and father to fashion Wisconsin's largest general contractor and construction management concern. Boldt is known for its quality work and innovative approach to building. In keeping with the family tradition, both of Oscar C.'s sons, Charles and Thomas, are active in the business.

Boldt has been nationally recognized among America's top contractors and construction managers by *Engineering News-Record*. A company of many talents, Boldt has built a foundation on its equipment. In fact, *Construction Equipment* magazine features Boldt as one of the nation's "equipment-owning giants."

Because of its unique capabilities, Boldt works throughout the country. This may include construction of hospitals, pulp and paper mills, and office buildings or sewage treatment plants. Boldt expertise has even been used as far away as Saudi Arabia.

The landmark list for just the Fox Cities is impressive: Lawrence University buildings, including the Music-Drama Center, Russell Sage Hall, and Downer Center; Aid Association for Lutherans headquarters and its downtown addition; W.A. Close; Gimbels; Appleton Center; Valley Bank Plaza; Appleton Public Library; Kimberly-Clark Corporation's research center, corporate headquarters, and other facilities; headquarters for Thilmany Pulp & Paper Company and Neenah Foundry; Appleton Medical Center; Armstrong High School; Appleton and Neenah YMCAs; and numerous other industrial, commercial, and institutional projects.

This old photograph, probably from the 1920s, shows a Boldt house construction project in Appleton.

THILMANY PULP & PAPER COMPANY

It was in 1883 that Oscar Thilmany, a young German immigrant, founded American Pulp Company in Kaukauna, the tiny ancestor of the giant Thilmany Pulp & Paper Company branch of the Hammermill Paper Company family.

The 18 employees of that fledgling enterprise produced six tons of box board and food containers a day. By 1888 it was the fifth of seven paper mills in Kaukauna, and in 1889 Thilmany renamed the venture Thilmany Pulp & Paper Mills. Its product lines were broadened to include newsprint and catalog paper.

In 1895 Thilmany received large orders for fruit and vegetable wrappers from Monroe Wertheimer of California, who would become its second president in 1902, the year after the company was incorporated. Glazed and waxed papers soon became key products.

One of the first sulphate (kraft) pulp mills in the United States was put into production by Thilmany in 1912, and it marked the beginning of the firm's integration of pulp, paper, and converting at one location.

Oscar Thilmany, founder of Thilmany Pulp & Paper Company.

Wertheimer pioneered glassine and grease-proof papers, used as candy wrappers and cereal box liners. This helped during the Depression, when employment was kept at about 800. In 1932 the workday was cut from eight to six hours so that 150 jobless workers could be hired.

Thilmany's waterproof paper was important to the war effort during World War II. One variety helped beat a fungus that ruined rations in the South Pacific.

By 1950 Thilmany had 1,305 employees and was the largest specialty kraft mill in the United States. Poly-laminated and poly-coated papers, from building paper to ice cream wrap, became increasingly important. By 1958 Thilmany was the only mill extant in Kaukauna.

The 1960s and 1970s saw plastic-coated and laminated products gain importance, and computers boosted the demand for carbonizing paper. Thilmany pioneered foil-mounting papers and vapor barriers. There were few markets where Thilmany was not a factor.

Family ownership ended in 1969, when Thilmany was merged with Hammermill of Erie, Pennsylvania. Oscar Thilmany's mill had grown into an organization with international standing. By the end of 1983 and the beginning of its second century, Thilmany's dream had been compounded into a giant with 1,800 employees.

The Thilmany Pulp & Paper Company in Kaukauna around the time of its incorporation in the early 1900s.

ZWICKER KNITTING MILLS

Walter, Arthur, and Dewey Zwicker (left to right), co-founders of the Zwicker Knitting Mills.

Before the end of the 19th century Robert Emil Zwicker, in his native Germany, invented the first machine that could knit a sweater. And as that century turned, in 1900, he took his idea and his family and left for the United States.

By 1905 Zwicker had made his way to Appleton and went to work for the Crescent Knitting Company, then at the corner of Oneida and Washington streets.

When that firm was sold in 1907, Zwicker started his own knitting mill at 808 West Wisconsin Avenue in Appleton, site of an old watch factory. Saxony Knitting Works was incorporated in 1910, with Zwicker as president. His son, Arthur, was vice-president. This company occupied a building at 122 North Richmond Street.

Saxony was dissolved in about 1914, and another son, Walter, purchased some of the machinery to operate his own mill. Walter's father and mother moved to Eagle River with the youngest son, Dewey, and continued the business on a small scale. Arthur, meanwhile, went to work for the Eagle Knitting Company in Milwaukee.

It was about two years later when Dewey joined his brothers Walter and Arthur in the Appleton business, and in 1919 the three were together in the enterprise, forming the Zwicker Knitting Mills.

In 1923 Zwicker purchased a building at 410 North Richmond Street in Appleton, which until this time had housed a saloon on the first floor, dance hall on the second, and owners' quarters in the back. The entire structure was converted to manufacturing. Through expansions and the construction of new facilities, Zwicker has been at the same address ever since.

Dewey Zwicker became president in 1929 after Walter was killed in an automobile accident. The company continued to expand, emphasizing its dedication to technical advancement.

Because of a tight wartime labor market a branch plant was started in Waupaca in 1945, and in the early 1950s a new building was constructed there at 810 North Churchill Street. That plant performs intermediate knitting and sewing operations as it has since its inception.

In 1960 Dewey Zwicker retired as president, and the then vice-president and sales manager, Lloyd Paul, became president and general manager.

Zwicker acquired Eagle Knitting of Milwaukee and its branch plant in Shawano in 1963. Eagle, at that time, manufactured headwear and apparel, but Eagle is now Zwicker's Apparel Division. Accessory production was transferred to Appleton in 1980.

Distribution changed during the 1970s from the use of jobbers as middlemen to direct sales to the retailer. This meant increased demand for warehousing in Appleton where over 200,000 square feet of space was acquired between 1969 and 1978.

In the late 1960s the concern acquired Hansen Knits, a major customer, and began to sell products

Some of the early employees of Zwicker Knitting Mills, which was founded in 1919.

under its own private label, using the Hansen name. The Hansen Division is now a leader in women's and children's accessories for fine department stores and specialty shops.

Zwicker also acquired foreign facilities: Haiti in 1973 and El Salvador in 1975. In 1980, however, the El Salvador plant was closed because of the internal strife in that country. These plants produced labor-intensive handwear products that

could not be competitively made domestically.

In 1980 Thomas A. Zwicker, grandson of Arthur Zwicker and a fourth-generation family member who had been on the board of directors, took an active role in the operation of the business and was elected president.

In addition, other third- and fourth-generation Zwickers are active in the company, and there are fifth-generation family members who have worked at the knitting plant as summer help.

Zwicker's total employment ranges

from 1,100 to 1,400, and of those, 550 to 700 are employed in Appleton, including seasonal help. Of its total sales, about 80 percent is accessories (Appleton, Waupaca, and Haiti) and 20 percent apparel (Milwaukee and Shawano).

The company has a strong commitment to research and development. Unique in the industry, it is known for designing and building its own machinery in the engineering tradition of its founding father, Robert Emil Zwicker. The firm today is known as the largest manufacturer of knit accessories in America.

TWIN CITY SAVINGS AND LOAN ASSOCIATION

It was a new type of business venture — a financial association — that a small group of Neenah businessmen gathered to organize on a late-November evening in 1893.

There was a need for a pool of funds that could be loaned to members who wanted to buy homes, this group agreed as they met in the little office of attorney M.L. Campbell on Wisconsin Avenue in Neenah. It was a need that was not being filled by banks, which then were reluctant to part with mortgage money for private homes.

The next day, November 24, 1893, the board of directors of The Twin City Building-Loan and Savings Association, as it had been named, met officially for the first time. They appointed F.T. Russell as president. Russell, one of the incorporators of the association, also was president of the Russell Paper Co., which would later become Neenah Paper Co. Russell was given the duty of administering the association's assets, which amounted to $150 cash, the proceeds of the sale of 250 shares of stock at 60 cents a share to the charter members.

Finally, on February 20, 1894, the association, backed additionally by a $300 loan from two charter members, made its first mortgage loan. N.C.

Coats borrowed $485 to build a home in Neenah.

This was the beginning of decades of steady growth. By January 20, 1928, the association had assets of more than $150,000, and its name was shortened to Twin City Building and Loan Association. This reflected the primary accent of the association during the 1920s and would characterize its function in the mid-1930s and 1940s when burgeoning

The Twin City Savings and Loan Association main office, 108 East Wisconsin Avenue, as it appears today.

The 100 block of West Wisconsin Avenue at the turn of the century. The large building at the far left housed the law office of M.L. Campbell where Twin City Building-Loan and Savings Association was formed on November 23, 1893.

Fox Valley industry sparked a rapid growth in the demand by workers for new homes.

The institution became Twin City Savings and Loan Association in 1952. It had assets of over $4.1 million, and the accent had shifted to the importance of saving for the future of the postwar generation.

Back in 1893, the association had little need for office space, but over the years that changed dramatically. In 1967 a second office was built, in Menasha, another in Neenah in 1974, and the fourth in Appleton in 1980. By 1984 its assets exceeded $121 million.

Twin City Savings and Loan Association's main office, completed in 1965, remained on Wisconsin Avenue as it always had, just down the street from the spot where Campbell's law office once was.

HOME MUTUAL INSURANCE COMPANIES

Julius Bubolz founded the Farmers' Home Mutual Hail, Tornado, and Cyclone Insurance Company of Seymour, Wisconsin, with this farmhouse the firm's original headquarters. Forerunner of Home Mutual Insurance Company, the firm issued its first policy on May 1, 1900.

Home Mutual's early history and subsequent years represent the best of the American Dream.

From one room in a small farm home, and offering only one policy, the venture has grown and expanded to four companies operating in a six-state area providing a variety of insurance products and financial services.

The original idea developed from the wreckage of the 1899 Great Tornado, which caused massive damage and loss of life. Although many were concerned and had been affected by this storm, Julius Bubolz determined a plan that could ease their financial burden. A local leader, well respected for his ideas and service to the community, Julius gathered his neighbors together and explained his plan: a mutual wind insurance company, to which each member would contribute and from which losses would be paid. Within two months of the original meeting, 135 farmers joined the charter group, naming the new enterprise the Farmers' Home Mutual Hail,

Tornado, and Cyclone Insurance Company of Seymour, Wisconsin.

The firm issued its initial policy on May 1, 1900. The first employees of the new company were the Bubolz children who, in addition to daily farm chores, handwrote the policies.

The company prospered. In 1926 the name was shortened to the Home Mutual Hail, Tornado Insurance Company. By 1931 the firm had grown to a point where it needed larger, more convenient quarters and additional personnel. The Irving Zuehlke Building was selected and served as corporate headquarters for 21 years.

The 1930s were difficult years. The Great Depression, catastrophic tornadoes, and a changing business climate provided great challenges as well as great opportunities. To answer the need for automobile insurance, the Home Mutual Casualty Company was formed in 1935. Within a few years this new organization surpassed the parent company in premium growth.

By 1941 the parent company, now renamed the Home Mutual Insurance Company, broadened its product line to include dwelling and business

The firm's home office is in Appleton, Wisconsin.

coverage.

Operations were started in the neighboring states of Minnesota, Michigan, Indiana, and Missouri between 1947 and 1957; Iowa was added in 1971. Expanding company operations and more personnel dictated other moves: in 1951 to the Aid Association annex and then, in 1963, to its own home office building.

As new product lines developed, companies were organized or merged from past operations. The Homestead Mutual Insurance Company was formed in 1956 to handle all farm lines; Home Mutual and the Casualty Company merged in 1952, writing all non-farm business other than life insurance. To consolidate operations, Homestead Mutual merged with Home Mutual in 1973.

To provide increased security through total financial planning, three organizations were established: Homeco Life Insurance Company in 1966; Homeco Securities, Inc., in 1968; and Homeco Financial Corporation in 1974.

Today the Home Mutual Companies look forward to the future, applying the basic principles set forth many years ago: "That our corporate responsibility is to serve humanity, giving direction and vitality to our companies' progress and growth."

FIRSTAR CORPORATION

Founded in 1870, First National Bank moved from rented quarters one year later to this building on the southwest corner of College Avenue and Appleton Street in Appleton.

Appleton was a thriving city of 4,518 in 1870, and Augustus Ledyard Smith was its mayor. Smith had been a banker for two years, too, so it was not surprising that he was the leading organizer and the first president of the First National Bank, which opened that year.

In 1868 Smith had started a private bank, and so greatly had it prospered that he decided to reorganize it as a national bank.

The 12 shareholders in Smith's bank met on November 14, 1870, to create the First National Bank. A week later it opened for business in rented quarters on the second floor of the Pettibone-Peabody Building on the northeast corner of College Avenue and Appleton Street in downtown Appleton, assuming $60,000 in deposits and $30,000 in loans and discounts from Smith's bank.

Within a year the bank constructed its own two-story building on the southwest corner, across from the rented offices. That facility, which opened on December 6, 1871, served for the next 43 years, until a magnificent Greek Revival structure was erected on the northwest corner of Appleton and College. The cornerstone for that building was laid on August 18, 1913, by John Fellion, the man who did the same masonry for the first structure.

First National continued to grow, to the point that it was able to successfully weather the Great Depression's famous banking holiday in 1933.

Eventually, the grand old building became cumbersome and crowded, and a new one was erected on the same site. It opened in November 1964.

In 1965 First National was recognized by the Federal Reserve System as a bank holding company to acquire stock of First National and Valley National banks.

Planned expansion began in 1970 with the additions of Freedom State Bank, First National Bank of Seymour, and First National Bank of Clintonville. Community Bank of DePere became a member bank in 1974; Farmers State Bank of Larsen and First State Bank of Campbellsport, affiliates in 1976 and 1978, respectively; and Oshkosh National Bank, a member in 1979.

Finally, in 1983, this broad-based financial organization became Firstar Corporation, reflecting the greatly increased scope of the bank that Augustus Smith had founded more than 100 years before.

Still at College and Appleton but on the northwest corner, First National laid the cornerstone for its second home in 1913. This Greek Revival building stood until 1964, when today's headquarters was constructed on the same site.

GIMBELS

How Gimbels happened to come to the Fox Cities is an unusual story. When Appleton's old Geenen's store closed in 1966, a civic group searched for a department store to co-anchor a refurbished College Avenue. By sheer oversight, Gimbels wasn't on the list.

Then, in 1967, a member of the group went to Milwaukee to see the Mayfair Marshall Field's manager. By chance, he was out of town. The company's first modern store on a downtown main street.

Gimbel Brothers traces its history not to New York City, but to Vincennes, Indiana. There, in 1842, Adam Gimbel shed the peddler's pack he had carried for the seven years since he emigrated from Germany, and opened a small store and trading post.

The first full-fledged Gimbels city's first radio station, the first escalators, the first 40-hour retail work week, and Wisconsin's—and Gimbels'—first shopping center branch, at Milwaukee Southgate, in 1954. Mayfair opened in 1958, and in 1962 Gimbel Brothers acquired a major Milwaukee rival, Ed. Schuster & Co.

A rapid 1970-1972 expansion added four stores in 22 months:

Gimbels Fox Cities, located at 122 East College Avenue in Appleton, is the company's first modern store on a downtown main street.

Appleton man stood wondering what to do. He glanced south, spotted Gimbels, and on impulse called on the manager. He was taken to meet an executive involved in site selection and familiar with the Fox Cities.

There followed, of course, many discussions, but on March 11, 1971, Gimbels Fox Cities opened, the department store wasn't in New York, either, nor in Vincennes. In 1887 the buildings there were sold, Adam Gimbel retired, and six of his seven sons moved to booming Milwaukee to found Gimbel Brothers.

The store began expanding almost immediately. By 1901 construction had begun on the first of five new store segments. Success there led to stores in Philadelphia, New York, and Pittsburgh. A 1923 merger united Gimbel Brothers and Saks & Co.

Milwaukee's first Gimbels had the Milwaukee's Southridge and Northridge, Madison's East Towne—and Gimbels Fox Cities.

In 1973 Gimbel Brothers became a subsidiary of B.A.T Industries of London, whose operations include tobacco, retailing, paper, cosmetics, and other enterprises. Gimbels, along with Saks Fifth Avenue, is now part of the retail division of BATUS Inc., B.A.T's U.S. holding company. Others include Kohl's Department Stores, Marshall Field, and Thimbles stores.

ST. ELIZABETH HOSPITAL

The only hospital in Appleton in 1885 was a converted house run by a doctor who, according to rumor at the time, was less than scrupulous. It was this that prompted community leaders, led by Mayor Hamilton A. Levings, to appeal to the Franciscan Sisters of the Sacred Hearts of Jesus and Mary to establish a hospital in their city.

It took 14 years, however, before there were sufficient resources. Sisters Carola, Armella, and Clothilda arrived in Appleton from St. Louis, Missouri, on November 19, 1899, the Feast Day of St. Elizabeth. It was only fitting that their new hospital be named for this saint who had been canonized for her service to the sick in Europe.

The new hospital found its first, temporary home in an eight-room residence at 110 East Fremont Street.

In the hospital's Pulmonary Rehabilitation Department, athletes can measure the amount of oxygen their bodies use to determine their exercise tolerance. This is the same test utilized by Olympic athletes to measure their cardiopulmonary fitness.

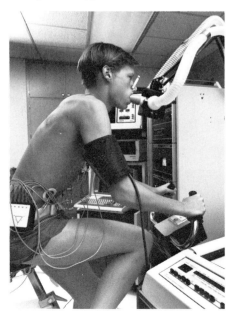

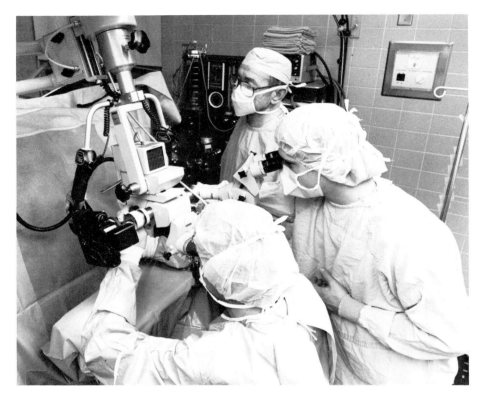

Microscopic neurosurgery is another of the high-technology procedures available at St. Elizabeth Hospital.

The eight rooms were for the patients; the Sisters lived in the attic. The makeshift kitchen was the place where the Sisters recited their morning prayers. It also was the dining room, workroom, and, when the need arose, the operating room.

The Sisters prepared all the food, most of which they raised, for the patients, the staff, and themselves. They kept sheep and chickens, an apple and plum orchard, and a grape arbor, as well as tilled a large garden. Into the 1940s, before expansion took over the land, the gardens were popular with the Sisters and the patients.

In the 18 months that the Fremont Street house served as a hospital, 108 patients were treated. Of those, 95 had surgery. The first surgical patient was Thomas Nooyen. Sister Clothilda admitted him, prepared him for surgery, watched as he awakened from the anesthetic, and was back scrubbing floors and cleaning soon afterward.

The Sisters bought eight acres adjacent to their first hospital, and in 1900, with $8,734 in donations from the community, construction started on a new, two-story brick building. It opened early in 1901 with 50 beds, a surgical suite, an X-ray machine, a laboratory, a pharmacy, and a laundry.

But the community grew rapidly, and by 1920 the hospital was woefully inadequate, with 70 beds jammed into a facility meant for 50.

Despite similar pleas to the Franciscans from other midwestern hospitals, the Sisters' order agreed to furnish $200,000 for an expansion — if the people of Appleton would contribute $300,000. Twenty-six doctors organized a campaign through

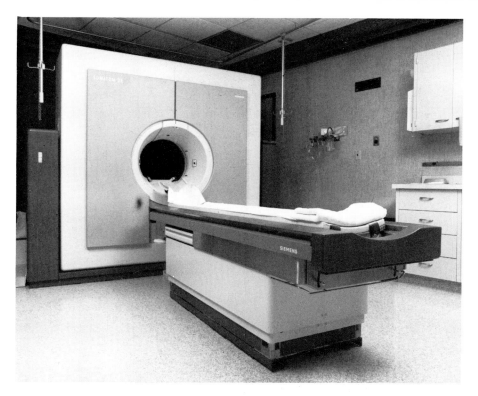

An advanced C-T (computerized tomography) scanner was added to the hospital's radiology services.

the *Appleton Post-Crescent*, and the funds were raised in four days.

The cornerstone was laid in October 1921, and when the hospital was completed in 1923 the five-story, red brick building could care for 200 inpatients. In 1924, 270 babies were born at St. Elizabeth.

In the years to follow, there was remodeling and expansion as needed. But in 1962, St. Elizabeth Hospital's needs were again outgrowing its facilities. After two years of planning, ground was broken in 1964 for a $9-million expansion and modernization program.

In the summer of 1966 a new, five-level south wing addition was occupied, with the top four levels devoted to patient care. That same year a new three-level east wing, housing X-ray, laboratory, emergency, outpatient, and special studies departments, was completed and occupied.

That original 50-bed hospital was razed, and in its place a three-level building was erected, with the ground floors built and furnished as quarters

for the Sisters, with recreation, dining, study, and community rooms and a library.

During 1967 and 1968, most of the expansion and modernization program was aimed at updating the hospital

building erected in 1924 to accommodate a cafeteria and various therapy departments. The entire program was completed and dedicated by the end of 1968.

St. Elizabeth now has more doctors on its staff than there were patients in that first year. With more than 330 beds, it offers patients services that range from alcoholism treatment to microscopic neurosurgery, with everything from biofeedback to home care in between. St. Elizabeth Hospital is constantly growing and updating its services and facilities to meet the changing health care environment of the 1980s.

St. Elizabeth's 18-million-electron volt linear accelerator provides sophisticated cancer treatment for 25 patients each day.

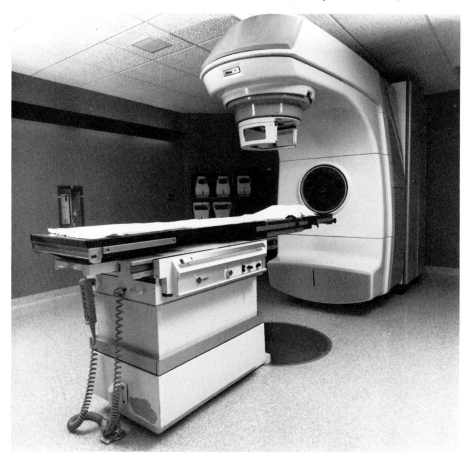

FOX VALLEY TECHNICAL INSTITUTE

The Appleton campus of the Fox Valley Technical Institute was completed in 1972 on a 142-acre site in northwest Appleton. The district headquarters is at this location.

The diverse areas of the Fox Cities had long-standing commitments to vocational and adult education that variously went back to the turn of the 20th century, but it was in 1967 that they first fell under one auspice, the Fox Valley Technical Institute.

In 1962 Congress passed the Vocational Education Act, which allocated funds to the states for vocational, technical, and adult education. To administer this, the Wisconsin Board of Vocational, Technical and Adult Education was created.

In turn, the Wisconsin Legislature in 1965 decreed that all areas of the state must fall in a local district by 1970. Traditionally, vocational education had been a local endeavor.

The Fox Valley Vocational, Technical and Adult Education District, comprised of 25 public high school districts, was created in 1967, one of 16 such districts in the state.

Situated 20 miles from the main campus, the Oshkosh campus began offering classes in its new facility in 1982. This facility recently received state and national recognition for its energy-efficient design.

William Sirek was the district's first administrator. He retired in 1982 and was replaced by Stanley Spanbauer, Ph.D.

Changes left the district with its present 26 member school districts: Appleton, Brillion, Chilton, Clinton-ville, Freedom, Hilbert, Hortonville, Iola-Scandanavia, Kaukauna, Kimberly, Little Chute, Manawa, Marion, Menasha, Neenah, New London, Omro, Oshkosh, Seymour, Shiocton, Stockbridge, Waupaca, Wautoma, Weyauwega, Wild Rose, and Winneconne.

The first phase of the district's building program was completed in 1972 on a 142-acre site at the northwest edge of Appleton, with the health and social services building added in 1973 and the diesel, farm

Many students do a portion of their work on computer terminals. It is projected that by 1985 all faculty, staff, and students will be computer literate.

machinery, and truck shop completed in 1974.

FVTI was created with the philosophy that "there should be equal educational opportunity for all the people of the district. All citizens must be given the opportunity to develop their capabilities to the fullest possible extent."

While continuing to expand the Appleton campus, FVTI began also to reach out to its students, establishing regional learning centers.

Twenty miles from the main campus is the Oshkosh campus. The 66,000-square-foot facility received state and national attention for its energy-efficient design. It serves about 13,000 students annually.

In 1967 the district opened the Neenah-Menasha center, where about 4,700 students take classes.

The Wautoma Regional Learning Center opened in 1978, and it serves about 1,900 students a year.

Approximately 2,200 students are trained each year by the Clintonville center, which opened in 1979.

The fifth regional center, in Chilton, began operation in 1980, serving about 2,000 students.

The Appleton campus, which is the district headquarters, includes business education laboratories, nursing labs, agribusiness labs, a truck-driving school, electromechanical and computer labs, and food-service facilities that rival the best in the nation.

In addition, evening classes are also offered in the 26 high schools in the district.

Total enrollment of the Fox Valley Technical Institute is almost 6,000 full-time students, and there were more than 47,000 people who took at least one course from the district in 1983. About 1,200 full- and part-time instructors are needed.

FVTI points to the fact that "the

only entrance requirement is the desire to learn." Its classes range from personal enrichment to full-fledged, highly technical career programs, from training students for their first jobs to upgrading the skills of people already employed. Students range in age from 16 to 75.

The school district offers associate degree programs in 27 fields, from accounting to technical nursing. Vocational diploma certificates are awarded in 30 separate occupational specialties, and it has the responsibility for formal apprentice training for 24 vocations.

The district's budget has grown to $21.6 million for 1983-1984. It derives half of this from local property tax. Most of the remainder comes from state and federal aids and from student fees.

But ultimately, it is the students who are a measure of the district's success. More than 82 percent of the 1,251 students who graduated in the 1982-1983 school year and are in the labor market are employed.

VOITH, INC.

Machinery has always been the business of the enterprise known now as Voith, Inc. It was started as a small machine and blacksmith shop in Appleton in 1883, Valley Iron Works, making milling machinery, waterwheels, and other machinery.

The company fell on hard times, however, and went into bankruptcy in 1897; the next year it was taken over by E.A. Peterson, who had been its superintendent. The Peterson family subsequently was involved in the business for 75 years.

Valley Iron Works was incorporated in 1900 and developed into a manufacturer of pulp and paper-making machinery to serve the growing Fox Valley industry. Until

An early photograph shows Valley Iron Works at its former location in Appleton's industrial flats.

A workman stands beside a headbox, a section of a papermaking machine manufactured by Valley Iron Works, circa 1940.

about 1930, the firm's principal products were beating, screening, and refining equipment for the paper industry.

In the early 1920s Valley Iron Works became the licensed builders of the Voith Inlet, an important part of the fourdrinier type of paper machine. Up to this point, the company had produced cylinder paper machines. These began to fall from favor, bowing to the more productive fourdriniers. Until the Depression, orders poured in.

Having weathered those times, Valley Iron Works entered the war era. It was then that the firm participated in the Manhattan Project, producing pumps for caustic substances in the atomic bomb, an achievement for which it would later be cited.

In 1945, after the Voith patents had expired, Valley Iron Works began to produce its own inlet and headbox combinations. It made these and other paper-machine sections until it was decided in 1958 that the organization was ready to market its first complete machine. The first order, received late that year, went to Nicolet Paper Company of West DePere, Wisconsin, and the firm has continued to produce complete paper machines since that time.

Valley Iron Works was purchased by Allis-Chalmers of Milwaukee in 1959 and operated successively as a subsidiary, plant, or division until 1974, when Allis-Chalmers and J.M. Voith GmbH of West Germany operated the business as a joint venture called Voith-Allis. In 1977 Voith purchased Allis-Chalmers' share, and the organization became Voith, Inc.

In 1977 a new office and manufacturing facility was built in Appleton's Northeast Industrial Park, where it still produces papermaking machinery.

AIR WISCONSIN

This is one of Air Wisconsin's first aircraft, a deHavilland Dove, in a flight over the Fox Cities.

The conception of Air Wisconsin developed out of a community need. In the early 1960s, local Fox Valley citizenry harbored great concerns that their convenient airline service was in jeopardy. North Central Airlines (the predecessor of Republic) had petitioned the Civil Aeronautics Board to eliminate service at Outagamie County Airport. Involved community leaders determined that the only solution to local airline service was to take on an effort to establish the Fox Cities' own carrier.

It was on August 23, 1965, that Air Wisconsin literally got off the ground, a year and a half after it officially came into being. It was born "Fox Cities Airlines, Inc.," in December 1963. But before it could begin operations, public funding support had to be garnered. With successful subscriptions in place, the nation's first publicly held commuter airline was to be a reality.

A primary step that allowed the new airline to become airborne was the decision by the Outagamie County Board of Supervisors to spend $2.8 million—initially all local funds with no state or federal aid—on a new

airport. The board, planning it in concert with the Fox Cities Chamber of Commerce and Industry, purchased a site west of Appleton, constructed a runway, taxiway, hangars, and a small, prefabricated administration building.

With these primary factors resolved, the directors of Fox Cities Airlines voted to change the name to Air Wisconsin.

Then, in 1965, the new airline acquired two nine-passenger deHavilland Dove aircraft and on August 23, with three pilots, 17 employed in operations and management, along with a limited number of maintenance personnel, began nonstop service between the

Fox Cities and Chicago's O'Hare International Airport.

As Air Wisconsin grew, so did its aircraft needs. After the Doves, the airline progressed with deHavilland Twin Otters, Beechcraft 99s, and Fairchild-Swearingen Metros. Allowing for greater expansion, the airline was certified by the CAB in 1978. By 1984 the large regional airline had standardized with 50-passenger Dash 7s and 100-passenger 146 Jets.

During its first year Air Wisconsin transported 3,535 passengers. During 1983 the airline boarded 802,997 passengers and transported over 11,800 tons of cargo. The professional staff has grown to nearly 700, with corporate offices on the second floor of the modern Outagamie County Airport terminal, which was opened in 1974 and expanded in 1983.

Born with pride—Air Wisconsin's growth and financial success is reflective of community vitality.

Air Wisconsin boarded 3,535 passengers during its first year. During 1983 the airline transported 802,997 passengers and over 11,800 tons of cargo.

THE INSTITUTE OF PAPER CHEMISTRY

An early researcher uses an optical microscope at The Institute of Paper Chemistry in Appleton.

One of the current generation of students uses the institute's electron scanning microscope.

The State of Wisconsin chartered The Institute of Paper Chemistry exclusively as a graduate school in 1929. Since its founding, it has been affiliated academically with Lawrence University. But the institute belongs to the pulp and paper industry. Basic support is through member companies. Any firm manufacturing pulp, paper, or paperboard in the United States is eligible for membership. The members support the institute through dues, which vary according to the size of the organization. Support is also derived from nonprofit contract research by the staff.

Significant features of the M.S. and Ph.D. programs are an interdisciplinary core of fundamental courses in science and engineering and a core of applied science and engineering courses putting the fundamentals to work on practical industrial problems.

Most graduates have accepted responsible positions in research, development, production, and management in many areas of the pulp and paper and related industries.

Research is an essential ingredient of the graduate school environment and research results are an important product of the institute's program. The major research effort is on projects funded by member dues and is directed toward major areas of need in the paper industry. Research projects, analyses, and services can be contracted by companies and institutions, either individually or as groups. Research performed by students in fulfillment of their degree requirements constitutes a significant portion of the total research effort.

Consistent with the mission of graduate education, the focus of funded and student research is on basic knowledge needed to establish the foundation for future developments by member companies. The relevance of these research programs to the major needs of industry continues to stimulate innovative developments which can be applied by the industry in a relatively short time.

The institute also plays a key role in the collection and dissemination of information. Its library contains the most extensive collection of books, journals, and other literature dealing with the science and technology of papermaking. The *Abstract Bulletin* is a monthly publication that covers worldwide literature of the pulp and paper industry and related fields. Annotated bibliographies covering a broad range of subjects are prepared and published by The Institute of Paper Chemistry, as well.

APPLETON WIRE DIVISION
Albany International

Appleton Wire Works was established in 1895 by William Buchanan, his sons Gus and John, and a brother-in-law, Albert B. Weissenborn, to weave belts of wire cloth for papermaking. John left in 1912 to form his own wire-weaving business in Canada. Reorganization gave Gus Buchanan and Weissenborn equal partnerships.

In 1938 Gus Buchanan and Weissenborn died within six weeks of each other, and Gus' son, William E. Buchanan, became president. Appleton Wire was a poor fourth in the fourdrinier wire industry then, but the leadership and innovations of William Buchanan's three decades as president made Appleton Wire the largest wire-weaving company in the United States.

Technical milestones hinged on patents that improved the process and the product. Three assigned to Weissenborn in 1906, 1910, and 1913 involved loom mechanization.

In 1934 a brazed seam had been

A group of wire-weaving looms along the Atlantic Street side of the plant, circa 1910. These looms were operated by hand, and the sheds were still being changed by foot treadles (the levers on the floor). Conversion began in 1906 from manual to mechanical looms based on improvements invented at Appleton Wire Works.

Appleton Wire Works, circa 1910. The large, tin-roofed building on the left is the original plant, built in 1895. The "L"-shaped addition, in background, was completed in 1910. Steam for motive power and heat, and also compressed air, was produced in the powerhouse in foreground.

developed by Weissenborn and Buchanan. An improvement of the brazed seam was patented to William E. Buchanan in 1933, and some of the most modern brazed seams were based on this invention. A significant breakthrough of the 1930s was the invention by L. "Nick" Weber of hollow shute wire, making it possible to weave cloth with both warp and shute strands in the same plane. This improved the smoothness and printability of paper made on these "monoplane" wires. Every major wire-weaving firm in the world was licensed under these patents. Buchanan was granted patents in 1942 for single- and double-twisted cable wires—an innovation that resulted in increased wire life for coarse-mesh wires. Chromium-plated papermaking wire was developed in 1965, and chromium-plating services were made available to competitors.

In 1968, after 25 years of experimenting, plastic fabric weaving and seaming was in full swing, mostly as plain weave and some semi-twill. Four-shed was in the experimental

stage. In 1971 major work was done on heat stabilization, and two years later trials of five-shed were under way. The first DUOTEX® fabrics (double-layer plastics) were introduced to the market in 1975. The firm was also offering treatments to resist contamination.

Appleton Wire Works went through a major reorganizational change in December 1968 when it joined Albany Felt Company, Albany, New York, to form Albany International. In 1983 this corporation subsequently bought out its stockholders, returned to private ownership, divested itself of non-papermaking interests, and is today the largest weaver of papermaking clothing in the world—and the key to that success is technical innovation.

PIERCE MANUFACTURING INC.

Dudley H. Pierce, founding president of Pierce Manufacturing Inc.

Eugene L. Pierce assumed the presidency upon his father Dudley's retirement in 1937.

Douglas A. Ogilvie has been president of the firm since 1957.

It was an old church building at Fremont and Jefferson streets on Appleton's southeast side that provided the first home for the company that later would become Pierce Manufacturing Inc. There Dudley H. Pierce set up shop in 1913, repairing autos and other vehicles.

Under the name Auto Body Works, Pierce and his father, Humphrey Pierce, in 1914 started building various truck and bus bodies to be mounted on Ford Model "T" and other truck chassis.

Early in 1917 the decision was made to erect a factory at a site on Pierce Avenue, on property owned by Humphrey Pierce, which he sold to the company. The main facility was 40 by 158 feet, with an adjoining "L" for the office facing Pierce Avenue. Another building toward Eighth Street, some 18 by 30 feet, was used as a blacksmith and forge room. The

following year another building was constructed south of the office, extending to Spencer Street, from Eighth Street.

The company was formally incorporated in October 1917 with Humphrey as principal stockholder and Dudley as first president. Gustav C. Seegar, another native of Appleton, completed the three-man board.

Auto Body Works' first catalog offered bodies and cabs that could be bolted onto the buyer's Ford Model "T" to convert it into any of a number of types of trucks. It boasted that they were constructed of maple, oak, and 20-gauge steel. The firm's standard color was dark olive green. The catalog added, "May be had in any dark color desired without additional cost, but if ordered in white or other light colors, an additional charge of $5 is made for

extra material and labor." Storm curtains and commercial body fenders were extras.

There were no high-salaried officers in the enterprise then. Seegar and Dudley Pierce each drew wages of $18 a week. They wanted the corporation to become well established and profitable. Auto Body Works also employed 10 other men and one woman.

When Humphrey died in 1919, Dudley H. Pierce became the controlling stockholder. He retired in 1930, but served as president until his death in 1954.

Auto Body Works stopped building bodies for the Ford Model "T" in 1925. By this time the company had branched out into bodies for other chassis such as Reo, Dodge, Chevrolet, Ford, and others, supplying customers throughout Wisconsin and Upper Michigan.

Under the supervision of Eugene Pierce, Dudley's son, who joined the firm in 1927 and took over the helm when his father retired, Auto Body Works started building bodies from steel. Four-Wheel Drive Co. of Clintonville opened a division in

The original Pierce Manufacturing Inc. plant is located at 315 South Pierce Avenue in downtown Appleton.

Appleton called Eagle Mfg. Co., making derricks and other equipment used by utility companies. In the early 1940s Auto Body Works began supplying the utility bodies.

From there, the firm branched out into beverage, bakery, beer, furniture, and refrigerated milk truck bodies. It was also at this time that Auto Body Works started manufacturing what would become a vitally important product—fire trucks.

In 1946 the company constructed a building on the site of the 1918 addition in order to accommodate larger trucks and the machinery and equipment necessary for handling steel.

Auto Body Works was approached in 1957 by W.S. Darley Co. of Chicago, Illinois, and Chippewa, Wisconsin, to produce fire truck bodies under that company's label. This association continued until 1970. Meanwhile, the concern discontinued its van business and concentrated on fire and utility trucks.

Eugene Pierce died in 1958, and Douglas A. Ogilvie, who had joined the company in 1948 as a sales engineer, was elected president and later became controlling stockholder. The corporate name was changed to Pierce Manufacturing Inc.

Working with the Pitman Company of Kansas City, Pierce in 1959 built its first of what would become a mainstay of fire-fighting— the "snorkel" and later the "squirt."

There were to be more expansions of the plant, and in 1977 Pierce constructed new general offices and assembly facilities in the town of Menasha just west of Appleton. Most of the metal fabricating takes place at the plant in Appleton.

Pierce Manufacturing's primary products are fire trucks and utility and emergency rescue vehicles. Though the businesses were not originally related, Pierce Manufacturing has acquired the rights to the name "Pierce Arrow." It has over 400 employees and is international in scope, producing more units a month—about 80—than any other manufacturer of such equipment.

The firm's corporate headquarters is at 2600 American Drive, Menasha.

209

NEENAH FOUNDRY COMPANY

William Aylward, Sr., had been in Neenah for 13 years in 1872, long enough to know about the good, rich soil of Wisconsin and long enough to know that the farmers who tilled this soil needed strong plows.

He had worked as a foreman at the Moore & Brothers Foundry for several years when, with two employees, he started his own foundry to make those plowshares, the Aylward Plow Works.

Soon the product line expanded to include sugar cauldrons, barn-door rollers, sleigh shoes, bean pots, and other cast-iron items. Quality took a high priority with Aylward. He would travel the 40 miles to the docks at Green Bay by ox cart for Swedish pig iron, which he believed essential to superior castings.

That early foundry was basic. The melting furnace, called a "cupola," was fired by coal. A horse walked in a circle to power a huge bellows.

It was long, hard work with limited output, but between 1875 and 1880 business improved and Aylward's three sons, William Jr., Edward Charles, and John, joined the business. In 1881 the first shop addition was built. The product line was expanded to include cast-iron stoves.

In 1904 the company manufactured the first of a product that would make it known around the world: manhole covers and sewer grates. It is not unusual for travelers to return with such comments as, "I saw one of your manhole covers in Paris."

William Aylward, Sr., the founder of the company, died in 1907, and the name was changed to Aylward Sons Co. at that time.

In 1918 Edward Charles moved his operation "out in the country" to the site now occupied by Plant 1 and now

William Aylward, founder of the Aylward Plow Works which was later to become Neenah Foundry Company.

surrounded by part of the city of Neenah. He changed the name to E.C. Aylward Foundry Co., and in 1919 his only son, Edmund John, joined the firm after returning from duty in France.

E.C. Aylward died in 1926, and Edmund John became senior partner and manager.

At that time, the plant was a low-ceilinged structure, 80 feet long and 50 feet wide. The floors were clay, and molten metal and coke-fired salamanders furnished the heat. The office was a one-room building next to the railroad tracks. There were 15 employees.

The muscles of men continued to furnish most of the power. Coke was unloaded with pitchforks, the cupola was charged by hand, molten metal was carried in ladles by the molder who "poured off" his own castings, and the castings were moved around by hand.

In 1928 the newly renamed Neenah Foundry diversified to produce industrial castings for the growing Fox Valley paper industry. The following year, however, the nation's economy plummeted, and with it, the fortunes of Neenah Foundry. But Edmund Aylward had faith. He mortgaged his home to keep operating and plowed profits back into the company. Then, as the 1930s wore on, WPA programs began to

The sugar cauldrons, barn-door rollers, and plowshares in this old engraving were early products of the Aylward Plow Works.

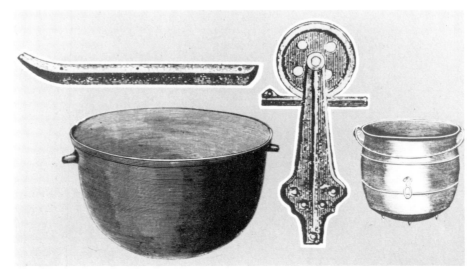

Manhole covers made in Neenah have shown up all over the world. This early one was made by the Aylward Sons Co., a predecessor of Neenah Foundry Company.

create a demand for manhole covers and construction castings. The company grew during the Depression, and its growth accelerated in the years following.

During World War II Neenah Foundry produced castings for the war effort. In 1946 the first automated molding lines were installed. By 1950 employment had grown to 320.

The eldest of E.J. Aylward's two sons, Edmund William, joined Neenah Foundry in 1948, and his brother, Richard John, graduated from the University of Wisconsin as a metallurgist and joined the business in 1953. He died suddenly in 1960.

E.J. Aylward became chairman of the board in 1959 and his son was elected president.

Plant 2 opened in 1960, the largest construction casting facility in the world. Employment had reached 565. Operations began at Plant 3 in 1967. This facility was designed to produce large industrial castings.

The foundry's capacity surpassed 800 tons a day, and employment exceeded 1,200. The catalog of construction products included more than 24,000 items, in use at such diverse locations as the Golden Gate Bridge, Disney World, the Empire State Building, Kennedy International Airport, and the St. Lawrence Seaway. The industrial division's range includes over 82,000 types of castings, from delicate dial indicators to 5,000-pound dam valves. There are more than 100,000 patterns in the company's warehouses.

It's a long way from simple plowshares.

Almost from the beginning, construction castings have been an important part of the firm's business.

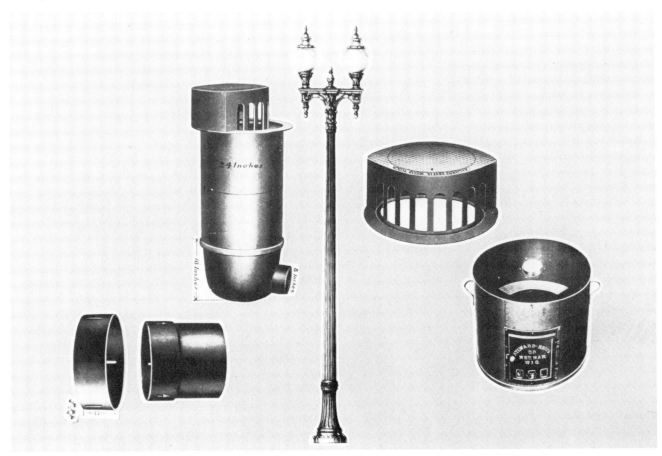

KIMBERLY-CLARK CORPORATION

Charles B. Clark, a young but astute businessman, was a junior partner in Leaven's Hardware Store in Neenah in the late 1860s. It was a place where the business of the community often was discussed. One of the topics was the then-new Smith & Van Ostrand Neenah Paper Mill, built in 1864.

Clark saw the potential of the paper industry, but had only $7,500, savings from Civil War military pay, which was about a quarter of what was needed for a new paper mill.

He went to John A. Kimberly and Havilah Babcock, who with Kimberly's brother Harvey were partners in a general store. John Kimberly and Babcock each were willing to put up a $7,500 share, and Kimberly suggested Frank C. Shattuck, a salesman for a Chicago dry goods firm, as the fourth.

Shattuck agreed, and the four young men—Clark was 28, Kimberly and Shattuck 34, and Babcock 35—began immediately to plan the new mill. Their enterprise, Kimberly, Clark & Co., officially came into existence on March 26, 1872.

Clark and Kimberly were designated active managers. They contracted for a paper machine that was installed and operating by October 1872, turning out two tons of all-rag newsprint a day.

Their plant, the Globe mill, substantiated Clark's belief in the growth potential of paper, and in 1874 the company bought out Smith & Van Ostrand. Kimberly, Clark & Co. expanded again in 1878 when it took part ownership and full management of the new Atlas mill in Appleton, which produced manila wrapping paper. Eventually the Atlas mill was sold to them.

In 1880 the partners incorporated as Kimberly & Clark Co., and in

1889 built a pulp and paper complex on the Fox River beyond Appleton, creating the community of Kimberly.

Then, in 1914, research led to a very significant event in the company's history: the development of "creped cellulose wadding," commonly known as tissue. This new product often was used in hospitals and aid stations as a substitute for cotton, which was in short supply during World War I. It was the ingenuity of Army nurses that adapted the material to what would become the firm's first consumer product—Kotex feminine napkins.

A related, second consumer product, Kleenex tissue, was introduced in 1924 for use in removing cold cream and makeup. It sold only moderately until it was marketed as a disposable handkerchief.

The company's present name, Kimberly-Clark Corporation, was adopted in 1928, when the stock was

The founders of Kimberly-Clark Corporation: (seated, left to right) John A. Kimberly, Havilah Babcock, (standing, left to right) Charles B. Clark, and Frank C. Shattuck. Kimberly, the last of the founders, died on January 21, 1928, after having served as president since 1880.

first offered to the public. K-C's first operations outside the United States were in Canada in the 1920s. After World War II came a period of rapid growth, with the firm acquiring or building facilities in a number of states and in other countries. Kimberly-Clark was well on its way to becoming a company which in 1983 had sales of over $3 billion and more than 32,000 employees worldwide, including about 4,600 in the Fox Cities.

Paralleling the company's early history are the contributions to the community by its founders and their families.

Kimberly helped start First

These were early boxes of Kleenex tissue before it was sold as a disposable handkerchief.

National Bank of Neenah and was on the school board for many years. Babcock was a director of First National and was active in the Presbyterian Church. Shattuck helped found National Manufacturers Bank and served for years on the Neenah Park Board. Clark was chief of the Neenah volunteer fire department, mayor for three terms, a state legislator, and was elected to Congress for two terms.

Clark's daughter, Theda, promoted public welfare projects and helped establish a library for which she donated the site. A memorial fund from her will provided the city's first hospital. Her brother, C.B., was responsible for her legacy being devoted to this project. He was a Neenah alderman, mayor, and school board member.

Mrs. Shattuck had a dump converted into a park which she gave to the city. The Shattucks' son, S.F., was on the park board and gave the land for the first high school athletic field. He was active in establishing a water utility and the Boys Brigade.

Babcock's daughters started a girls' club that developed into the YWCA. Kimberly's son, James, was on the first board of industrial education and gave the original family home to the Visiting Nurse Association.

Many of the succeeding Kimberly-Clark officers and their families were equally generous in their devotion to the community.

The four men who founded the company agreed in advance on a basic policy for the business. Among their principles were: manufacture the best possible product, serve customers well and deal fairly to gain their confidence and goodwill, and deal fairly with employees. These principles have continued to guide Kimberly-Clark through the years.

This is the heritage of a company that today operates in 19 states and 21 countries. Its well-known products are sold in 150 countries. As in the early days, K-C people have made the company grow by helping fill human needs and trying to build something better for tomorrow.

This was the original Globe Mill where Kimberly, Clark & Co. began operations in October 1872.

AUGUST WINTER & SONS, INC.

Even for 1928 it was a modest beginning when August Winter, who had been a fitter in Minneapolis since 1915, moved to Appleton and set up his heating business in a two-car garage at 413 North Bennett Street.

The fledgling venture grew steadily for Winter and his two sons, Roy and Walt, and in 1946, during the postwar building boom, the firm found need of larger quarters. A new facility, measuring 36 by 48 feet, was constructed at 1216 West Wisconsin Avenue. The company had five employees, one car, and a truck.

In 1953 the firm incorporated as August Winter & Sons, Inc. August retired that year, Roy became president, and Walter became vice-president. Annual sales were $256,400.

Winter & Sons' first out-of-state job, a $63,513 contract for heating

August Winter & Sons, Inc., is located in Appleton's Northeast Industrial Park.

work at a prison in Marquette, Michigan, was awarded in 1955. By this time the business had more than 40 employees, had completed the fifth addition to its building, and had a fleet of 14 vehicles.

Robert Gabel, who went to work for Winter & Sons in 1952, was licensed as a professional engineer in 1960, and the company added engineering to its fields of expertise. August Winter's grandsons, Thomas A. and Robert H., joined the firm full time in 1961, and plumbing and industrial work joined the repertoire.

In 1964 Winter & Sons was

awarded the heating, ventilating, and air-conditioning contract for the Aid Association for Lutherans' downtown building, at $933,000 its largest contract to date. In 1968 came the firm's first contract for piping a complete paper machine, for American Can Company of Roths-child, Wisconsin.

Growth was rapid in the 1960s, and in 1970 Winter & Sons moved to a new, 30,000-square-foot building in the Northeast Industrial Park. Walter Winter retired at this time, Roy became board chairman, and Gabel became president.

By 1973 Winter & Sons had become a complete mechanical contracting and engineering company. In 1980 Gabel became chairman of the board; Thomas Winter, president; and Robert Winter, executive vice-president.

August Winter & Sons, Inc., now has five professional engineers and six designers, with total employment over 200. It is listed among the top 100 mechanical contractors in the United States and is ranked fourth in Wisconsin. Sales for 1983 were about $25 million, with work being done in seven states, and the firm completed its third plant addition, larger itself than August Winter's original facility on Wisconsin Avenue.

The first headquarters of August Winter & Sons, Inc., was located at 1216 West Wisconsin Avenue in Appleton.

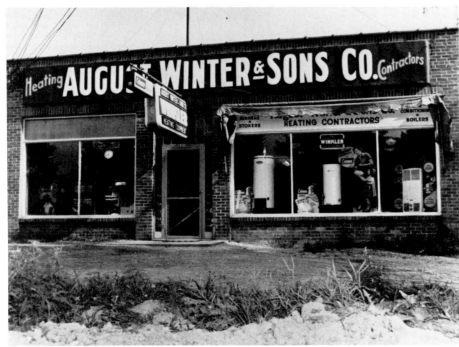

P.H. GLATFELTER COMPANY, BERGSTROM DIVISION

The flip of a silver dollar decided it. Dedrick W. Bergstrom and his brother, George, had come to Menasha from Norway as children. They had been partners in the Bergstrom Stove Company in Neenah for 25 years when, in 1904, they agreed that one should buy out the other's interest.

Dedrick lost the coin toss. And the stove company. But with what his brother paid him and with loans from friends, he purchased the Winnebago Paper Mills of Neenah from W.L. Davis and renamed the firm Bergstrom Paper Company.

At the time, the mill had two papermaking machines which made six tons of book paper a day from old rags and newspaper. Bergstrom Paper prospered sufficiently that an addition and another papermaking machine were added in 1912, and still another machine in 1919.

Dedrick Bergstrom died in 1928 at the age of 81, and his son, John Nelson Bergstrom, took over the company's top post. He held that job until he retired in 1948 and turned

over the reins to his youngest brother, Nathan.

In 1950 Bergstrom Paper acquired 450 acres of land west of Neenah that would in 1956 and 1960 become the site of a new finishing plant and offices.

Bergstrom Paper became a public corporation in 1955 with the sale of 70,000 shares of common stock, and in 1956 the firm bought Whale Safety Paper Co. of Waupaca.

Hugh R. Moore, son-in-law of Nathan Bergstrom, became president

The main office and converting plant of the P.H. Glatfelter Company, Bergstrom Division, is located on Bergstrom Road in Neenah.

of Bergstrom Paper in 1962. A $7.5-million addition and paper machine installation were completed in 1964.

There was more expansion with the purchase in 1969 of Tab Imprints of New York City and in 1970 of Cromwell Business Forms of Albany, New York. Bergstrom Paper doubled its size in 1972 by buying a Kimberly-Clark Corporation pulp and paper mill in West Carrollton, Ohio.

The fourth family member to be president of the venture was Dedric W. Bergstrom, who has held that post since 1975.

In 1979 Bergstrom Paper Company was merged into P.H. Glatfelter Company of Spring Grove, Pennsylvania, a manufacturer of printing and writing papers. Dedric Bergstrom, the grandson of the man who lost the coin toss, was named president of the division.

The firm's manufacturing plant, mill office, waste-treatment center, and bleachery plant at the Wisconsin Avenue, Neenah, location.

APPLETON PAPERS INC.

By the time Charles S. Boyd graduated from Lawrence College in Appleton in 1893, he was already pursuing a career in the paper industry—selling paper bags and wrapping paper to merchants.

After graduation, he began selling fine papers and, in 1905, he founded a paper company in his own name at Kaukauna.

But his paper industry pursuit really took wing in 1907 when he founded what would decades later become Appleton Papers Inc., the American papermaking arm of a huge international corporation.

It was in 1907—with an almost miniscule $14,100 in capital—that Boyd organized The Appleton Coated Paper Company, a key predecessor of Appleton Papers. By the end of that year, capital had increased to almost $17,000 and another $25,000 was added the following year.

In the early days, clay and casein

for coating paper were hand-mixed and transferred from tank to coating machine with a hand dipper. After coating, the paper was literally hung up to dry, draped above steam coils. These coaters were far cries from the high-speed, electronically controlled giants with enclosed drying chambers that were destined to serve the company decades later.

Boyd served as president of Appleton Coated from 1907 to 1945 and 1948 to 1952. He was chairman of the board from 1945 to 1952, when he died at the age of 80.

In the 1920s Appleton Coated

In 1917, ten years after its founding, The Appleton Coated Paper Company looked like this in Appleton. It was the primary forerunner of Appleton Papers Inc.

began to develop a line of mill-brand papers. Then, in the early 1930s, when paper machines were redesigned to make and coat paper in a single operation, the firm started to concentrate on coated specialties—bond, printing enamels, label papers, tag, and other products that were coated off the paper machine.

It was in 1953 that a major step was taken, the production of carbonless paper for The National Cash Register Company of Dayton, Ohio, later to become NCR Corporation. In 1954 came the pioneer marketing of carbonless paper, which was to become known as Appleton's NCR Paper* brand.

Two other predecessor firms were to become integral forces in the makeup of Appleton Papers: D.M. Bare Paper Co., born in 1867 in Roaring Spring, Pennsylvania; and Combined Locks Paper Co., founded in 1889 in Combined Locks, Wisconsin.

The founder and first president at the Pennsylvania pulp and paper mill was Daniel M. Bare. History would

Around 1920 the Locks Mill, then Combined Locks Paper Co. at Combined Locks, Wisconsin, was producing paper on this machine. The enterprise was founded in 1889.

Mike
Appleton Paper

and the building opened on July 1, 1974.

The 26 physicians from the two clinics brought with them all of their respective administrators and employees. There were 80,000 medical records to be merged into a single system.

The Nicolet Clinic's 1983 staff consisted of 42 physicians in 23 specialties, with three locations in the Fox Cities area and outreach programs in consultive specialty and sub-specialty services in five outlying community hospitals.

The third location, North Menasha, was opened in January 1982 at 878 Airport Road, with three physicians. That number soon grew to seven. All three locations have full laboratory and X-ray facilities.

As the clinic entered 1984, it was enlarging its building at 411 Lincoln Street to meet the growing needs of patients. The addition will house expanded laboratory, X-ray and ultra-sound services, and a new physical therapy service. An immediate-care service will also be part of the new addition, with services available to patients who must be seen immediately by a physician. The project was to bring eight additional physicians into the clinic in specialties not previously offered.

Nicolet Clinic saw an average of 950 patients a day in 1982, with a total of 230,000 patient visits for the year. There were 178 employees, and the clinic maintained 143,000 medical records. In 1983 Dr. Douglas Reilly was president of the clinic; Dr. David Hathaway, medical director; and Dale J. Anderson, administrator. They led the clinic as it continued to pursue what had always been its goal—high-quality medical care delivered in a cost-effective manner.

in 1962 and shortly thereafter were joined by four other doctors. In 1965 William Hildebrand's son, Dr. Fredric L. Hildebrand, joined the clinic, followed soon by three other doctors.

When the merger of the two clinics came, the staff of each seemed to complement the other. It was decided that one of the two Riverside buildings in Menasha would be retained and staffed and the other sold. Physicians from both clinics would occupy the new building in

Nicolet Clinic-Riverside, 515 Broad Street, Menasha.

Nicolet Clinic-North, 878 Airport Road, Menasha.

Neenah.

One of the many questions that had to be negotiated was the name of the new entity, since neither of the previous ones would have been appropriate. The name of the famous explorer, Jean Nicolet, was chosen,

THE R. SABEE COMPANY

Reinhardt Sabee had wanted to be in business for himself for a long time. It was this long-standing desire, combined with a truly uncommon ability to design manufacturing machinery, that led him to found his own firm, The R. Sabee Company, in Appleton in the early 1950s.

In 1951 Sabee left his job as a machine designer for the Kimberly-Clark Corporation and established offices at 230 South Linwood Avenue in Appleton.

Initially, the company's business was the design and construction of manufacturing machinery, much of it concerned with packaging and paper converting.

Sabee had developed a reputation throughout the paper and related industries as an innovator. He has been known not only for what the machines he has designed are capable of producing, but also for their ease of operation. They were designed to be operated by workers with a minimum of skill and training, rather than requiring the attention of an engineer, which is not uncommon elsewhere in the industry.

Product innovation and machine design have gone hand in hand for Sabee. For example, he developed a softer, more conformable disposable diaper. Sabee patented such a convenience product in the early 1950s. He holds patents on many forms of disposable diaper constructions.

For several years The R. Sabee Company designed and produced manufacturing machinery for other companies, including some of the biggest corporations in the country. Several companies have been licensed under Sabee patents, and the firm has a reputation for solving manufacturing problems.

Sabee also holds patents on techniques for creating so-called spun-bonded fabrics. This is one of the materials used in the manufacture of

Reinhardt Sabee founded The R. Sabee Company in Appleton in 1951. The company headquarters is still located at the original 230 Linwood Avenue location.

The Great Northern Corporation's head-quarters is at U.S. 41 and Stroebe Island Road in the Town of Menasha.

Advertising Council.

The company's ability to address the packaging market got additional strength when Great Northern Corporation formed an affiliate company, Laminations Corporation. This concern is involved in the manufacture, marketing, and distribution of V-Board and Contour.

V-Board is a protective shipping and packaging material designed especially to protect the edges of merchandise and the corners of containers from shipping damage, as well as adding structural strength.

Contour is a laminated material that is used extensively in the furniture industry. It can be constructed in a wide variety of shapes, including furniture, but it also is used in making heavy-duty shipping containers, as well as point-of-purchase displays.

Great Northern entered the plastics market in 1975 with the acquisition

of Robin Manufacturing Company, from the Parker Pen Corporation, which had a manufacturing plant in Markesan. Further penetration of the plastics market came in 1976 with the acquisition of The Molders, a Milwaukee-based manufacturer of custom-molded products.

These two were merged in 1978 into Great Northern Plastics, Inc., with headquarters and manufacturing facilities in Milwaukee.

This division was enhanced by an asset/stock exchange with Tuscarora Plastics, Inc., of New Brighton, Pennsylvania, in 1979. Tuscarora Plastics, in conjunction with Great Northern Corporation, manufactures and markets custom-molded polystyrene products in the Midwest, East, and South. With 14 manufacturing facilities and two technical centers, this arm of the business designs and produces protective packaging material of molded polystyrene to fit the configuration of a particular product. It also produces other specialty packaging such as thermoformed

"blister" boxes, gift cheese trays, and specialty food containers.

To expand its market capabilities, Laminations West, Inc., was formed as a joint venture in Los Angeles to provide manufacturing capability to supply West Coast customers. The company also produces a complete line of paper cores and tubes.

Since 1962, when Great Northern was formed, the times have changed for packagers. Even the name has been changed to Great Northern Corporation to reflect its broader interests.

The founders of the firm set out to manufacture and market what essentially were plain brown boxes with unsophisticated printing. But this has given way to creative graphics that help sell the product inside the container. Great Northern Corporation, which prides itself in solving difficult packaging problems cost-effectively, now uses sophisticated four-color lithographic printing and labeling capabilities to transform those plain brown boxes into billboards.

AMERICAN CAN COMPANY

Assembly of the organizations that would form the American Can Company began in 1927 when Marathon Paper Mills acquired Menasha Products Company, formerly Menasha Printing and Carton Company. Products included calendars and calendar pads, chewing gum wrappers, waxed paper for food packaging, paperboard boxes, wood and paperboard cheese boxes, and paraffined cartons. Local operations included a paper mill, wax refinery, art department, electrotype plant, engraving plant, and ink plant, along with converting operations.

Expansion was rapid and steady. Menasha got a new steam plant in 1928 and a new carton plant in 1929. In 1936 the firm bought Economy Paper Products Company of Milwaukee, and in 1940 transferred its equipment to Menasha. That same year a new office building was erected in Menasha, along with carton,

Operators at the firm's plastic ham can line.

An extruder operator works with hot molten plastic which will eventually become wrapping for various food products.

parafilm, and coating and laminating plants. It purchased the Whitmore Machine and Foundry Company, Menasha, in 1941 and operated it during World War II.

The venture's name was changed to Marathon Corporation in 1944. A new carton plant was built in Menasha in 1947, an ink plant in 1949.

In 1952 the Great Lakes freighter, D.C. Everest, was launched to economically transport pulp and raw materials between United States and Canadian operations.

Marathon Corporation was acquired by American Can Company in 1957, one year after a new Neenah plant had begun operation. The Neenah office building was completed in 1958. In 1962 the last paper machine in the Menasha Canal plant was dismantled and a new research and development and pilot plant was built in Neenah.

At present, the Neenah Technical Center conducts process and material research and product development. It includes testing facilities and a packaging machine laboratory.

Work at the Graphics Center in Neenah includes preparation of artwork, rotogravure cylinders, film, and flexographic printing plates.

The Neenah plant does printing and converts packaging products for several market areas. The Menasha plant, oldest of the Fox Cities operations, also prints and converts packaging material. The machine division in Menasha designs, modifies, and repairs equipment for manufacturing operations.